The Things That Saved Me

The Things That Saved Me

Breathing Light Into Our Stories

Melynne Rust

For my grandchildren,
Isla, Charlotte, Elizabeth, Harlynne, and James:
May you always glimpse threads of light in your story.

In glimpsing these threads of light amidst the weakness and distortions of my life let me be recalled to the strength and beauty deep in my soul.

— J Philip Newell, *Celtic Benediction*

Contents

Prologue

Stand Girl

Thread of Light: Remember your inherent worth

The summer I turned sixteen, I worked on a pick-your-own produce farm near Piscataway, Maryland, not too far from Washington, DC. People from the city loved coming down for a day trip, especially the older women who had grown up in the rural South, where everyone had their own vegetable garden out in the yard. I watched the transformation happen as they stepped out of their cars in the dirt parking lot, breathed in the fresh country air, and caught a whiff of their childhood memories. Tension slid off their shoulders. Creases faded from their faces. Wearing cotton frocks and straw hats with their cash tucked up in their ample bosoms, they climbed aboard the flatbed wagon hitched to the old rusty tractor and waited to be carried to the fields. To me, they were the embodiment of Mother Earth.

While they picked bushels of tomatoes, green beans, okra—

whatever was in season at the time—they reminisced about their old family homesteads and kinfolk. They debated the various methods for putting up their produce, from canning to freezing to pickling, but everyone agreed they wanted to capture that fresh-picked taste to enjoy in the colder months. I think they captured more than that. I want to believe that eating their preserved vegetables in the depths of winter reminded them of their connection with one another and with the land. I like to imagine it sustained them, grounding them, as the earth froze over and the hope of spring was a long way off.

When they came in from the fields, sweaty and spent, they bought themselves cold drinks from the Coke machine, wiped their faces with their handkerchiefs, and leaned solidly against the horseshoe-shaped checkout counter in the middle of the dirt-floored, pavilion-like farm stand. Regaining their equilibrium, they retrieved their money, limp with cleavage moisture, while we stand girls assessed their bounties and calculated what they owed.

I began working there shortly after I started dating the boy who would one day become my husband. He had recently been hired as a farmhand and told me they were looking for girls to run the stand. I was not yet sixteen, wouldn't be until later that summer, so I was too young for most of the jobs available to teenagers. I thought this would be a great way to make some money and maybe catch a glimpse of my new boyfriend during work hours.

The farmer's wife who interviewed me wasn't bothered by my age, but she told me she had already hired some girls to work in the stand and didn't think she needed anyone else.

Maybe it was the disappointment etched on my face or the way the air seemed to seep out of my body that made her reconsider. She said, "You know what? I could probably use you in the stand one day a week, to give the regular girls a break. And on the other days, you can always do piecework. If you'd be up for that?"

I had no idea what she was talking about, but I grabbed on to it. "Yes, ma'am! I'd love to do that." I let out a long breath. "Thank you!"

Piecework, I came to find out, referred to getting paid by the piece of whatever entity was custom for collecting particular produce. Like *flats* of strawberries, which is where I started, since it was peak season. I worked in those strawberry fields from sunup to almost sundown for the first few weeks. I started the day straddling a row of plants and bending over to pick the berries, but soon my back ached and my hamstrings felt tight. Then I squatted between the rows, but it didn't take long for my quads to start burning. Then I lowered myself to a kneeling position, with my shins in the dirt and my butt on my heels, scooting myself along the rows as I picked, counting the hours until our lunch break. Not exactly what I thought I had signed up for.

After strawberry season waned, we moved on to other produce. I loved picking tomatoes because it was easy to fill up a bushel basket with the large, succulent fruit. But the smell of a random tomato rotting in the hot sun was enough to make me swoon with nausea. The green beans, along with lima beans and garden peas, were my least favorite because they took so long to fill the basket. As I dropped them in, they seemed to echo like they'd fallen down a deep well, and it felt like the pile would never reach the top. The okra was way too itchy. And the greens! So many kinds of greens—collards, mustard, rape, kale—that it took me forever to tell the plants apart. Back then, the only way people talked about greens was how they would cook them down (boil or steam) with or without fatback. No one in my sphere had yet considered that kale could be eaten raw in a salad.

Suffice it to say that my one day a week filling in as a stand girl felt like I had won the lottery.

I had obligated myself to work the entire summer, but by the time July turned into August and another scorching month stretched ahead of me, I wondered if I had made a mistake. I was tired of picking vegetables. I was tired of the long hours. I was tired of being hot. And I was tired of being tired. For probably the first time in all my years of summers, I couldn't wait for September to show up and school to start up so I could stop working.

But by the following spring, I had committed to work another season. Somehow the land had gotten under my skin. I missed being near it. And after being cooped up in classrooms all year, I wanted to be out in the fresh air and feel the sun on my back, the breeze in my hair, the dirt in my hands. I wanted that feeling of connection that came to me when I was close to the earth.

My second summer I became a regular stand girl; I had paid my dues. I was still exhausted at the end of the long days, but it was a different kind of exhaustion. We didn't have cash registers, just simple cashboxes, so we had to calculate everything by hand. Our scales to weigh the produce were also the old-fashioned kind, so if the amount purchased was not in whole pounds, we'd have to eyeball how much was there and how much that cost. Math was not my best subject in school.

That second summer, I learned how to drive the farm truck, which had a gear shift extending from the steering wheel (*on the column*, they called it). Although I had learned how to drive a car with manual transmission, this was an entirely different beast. I never quite got the hang of it without stalling. I also learned how to drive the tractor that towed the flatbed wagon full of people to the fields. The tractor gears seemed more straightforward to me than the "on the column" shift, but there were other things to worry about. Like making sure I made wide turns on the narrow dirt roads between the fields so I didn't mow down any produce. And I couldn't go too fast or people might fall off, but if I went too slow the tractor might stall. It took me a while to feel comfortable enough that my heart rate didn't shoot up every time I sat down in the worn metal seat of that old rusty tractor.

We stand girls were not exempt from picking produce when the need arose. The pieceworkers usually kept the stand stocked for customers who stopped in for some fresh produce for dinner or maybe a few meals at the most. But occasionally someone came in and wanted an entire bushel of beans already picked, and we'd scramble to scrape together all the beans we had left in the bin.

Then one of us would have to go out to the green bean field and pick another bushel or two. We picked right alongside our pick-your-own customers, like the ladies in the cotton frocks with the straw hats. I loved listening to their conversations as their voices floated over the field. I admired how they seemed so at home with themselves.

At the end of every summer, I announced it was my last season. But every spring I would find my way back. The land kept calling my name. The land and the wind and the elements of the earth. The rhythm of the season, waking before the sun and working in its light as it ambled across the sky. And once the day was done and we could rest in the shade of the deep evening, the moon would let us know she was there too.

The summer I turned twenty years old was my fifth season working on the farm, and unbeknownst to me at the time, it would come to be my last. For you see, the young farmhand and I had fallen in love over those five summers, and after heading back down south for my third year of college that fall, I would find myself engaged by Thanksgiving, married in May, and living in downtown Chicago before I saw my next birthday. A lot of changes were ahead of me that took me far away from the land I had come to know and love.

But those years on the farm, so close to the land, left an indelible mark on my spirit, an imprint on my soul. It became a creed I carried in the memory of my bones: *I may be mere dust, but I am connected to a universe that celebrates dust, that grows new life out of the dirt every single day.* In the years to come, when I would be forgetting who I am, Mother Earth would always find a way to remind me of this sacred truth. Of my inherent worth. And it saved me, grounding me, when I was in the depths of my own personal winters with the earth frozen over and the hope of spring still a long way off.

Chapter 1

The Drowning Armadillo

Thread of Light: Believe you can tackle hard things

I t happened just after five o'clock on a Wednesday afternoon in the middle of August. It was the hottest time of day in the hottest month of the year in Florida, especially when your backyard faces west. I know this because every day at five o'clock, I fed my Labrador retrievers—Chocolate Bear and Black Skye—their dinner, then took them out back to do their business. I sweated profusely in the thick heat, but I couldn't trust them out there unaccompanied, as Skye had developed a bad habit of eating her poop if I didn't immediately scoop it up.

I wore a sleeveless linen dress that day, one with side pockets. With my hair tied up in a ponytail as usual, I tried hard not to sweat. I was meeting my son, Wilson, for dinner and didn't want to go to the trouble of changing my outfit. This is how I remember it was a Wednesday: because Wilson and I went to Bonefish Grill every Wednesday evening, starting January 6th of that year. In the Christian tradition, January 6th is the Day of Epiphany, which marks the revelation of the Christ child to the wise men who had followed a star to find him. That particular year, January 6th was also the day my husband of thirty-three years announced he wanted a divorce.

We'd been sitting in the office of our marriage counselor, just beginning our session with her, when Jay blurted this declaration. I don't know how long I sat there before I could respond. I only know it was after my ears stopped ringing, after the whooshing of wind in my head subsided, after the blood flow to my heart resumed, after I could trust my voice to actually utter a coherent sound.

"I'm not getting divorced three months before our daughter's wedding" were my first words.

How could he even contemplate bringing this up three months before Meredith's wedding? How could he contemplate bringing this up at all?

We had been in marriage counseling the past five months. I had presumed we would continue to be in marriage counseling for months after the wedding. We were working on things. The counselor had us reading a book, and we were engaging in relationship exercises she had given us. In my mind, we were in the middle of the *working it out* phase. Up to this point, neither one of us had mentioned the word *divorce* to the other.

I was stunned. Disoriented.

"I will not be shopping for a divorce attorney at the same time I'm shopping for mother-of-the-bride dresses," I continued. Meredith and I had plans to go shopping that very weekend. I crossed my arms over my chest. "I won't do it."

He stared at me, apparently not having considered he would receive any pushback—which was understandable. Over the long haul of our marriage, I think he had become accustomed to not receiving pushback from me.

"Uh," piped up the counselor, "perhaps a separation might be the way to go. For now."

I'd forgotten she was in the room.

It was later that night, as I sobbed myself to sleep, that I remembered the date. January 6th. *How ironic that this day will forever mark the revelation that my husband no longer wants to be tethered to me,* I thought.

It was my very own day of epiphany.

By the time August rolled around, I was neck-deep in the muck and muddle of everything entailed in dissolving a thirty-three-year marital union, including the selling and packing up of our beloved family home. I had wanted desperately to keep it, but with Jay gone and the three kids grown and out of the house (April, the youngest, was all the way down in Argentina), it had begun to feel too big for me to rattle around in alone. As much as I loved this home, the once-cherished memories now haunted me.

On that steamy August day, following the dogs into the backyard, I walked over to the sparse shade of the pool umbrella while keeping my eye on Skye. Bear trotted over to the bushes by the back fence, his nose in the air. He started pawing at something. It was an armadillo, I discovered, as it tore from its hiding place and dashed across the lawn with Bear in pursuit. Skye soon joined in, and together they chased the armadillo, who was barely holding on to a breath of a lead, through the yard.

I stood in my piece of shade and idly watched them, not the least bit concerned for the armadillo. They were a common sight in Florida and usually scurried into narrow spaces too small for Labradors. Also, I wasn't going to let myself sweat. I pulled my phone out of my dress pocket to check for messages, confident the armadillo would find his safe place soon, the dogs would give up the chase and take care of their business, and we could all go inside and cool off.

When I looked up, I was startled to see the armadillo heading straight for the pool. Surely, he'd veer in another direction. But to my alarm, he leapt right in and started swimming around the perimeter of the pool, frantically looking for a way out. For some reason, the dogs didn't jump in after him but chose instead to stir themselves into a frenzy on the pool deck, yapping and nipping at the armadillo as he valiantly tried to keep himself from drowning while not getting devoured.

I let out a sigh and slid my phone back into my pocket. I was going to have to do something about the ruckus.

I needed to get the dogs away from the armadillo before they jumped in the pool after him, but with no one there to help me, I couldn't just pull them away. They were too strong and crazy wound up. An idea came to me. I ran inside and snatched the box of Milk-Bone dog biscuits, ran back out, and started shaking the box, shouting above the melee, "Bone! Bone! Who wants a bone?"

That grabbed their attention. They looked at me with their heads cocked and ears perked, then looked back at the pool. Bone or armadillo? I shook the box more vigorously, sweat dribbling down the sides of my face, and yelled again, "Let's get a bone!"

The temptation for a sure thing was too much, and they ran over to me, scampering up the back porch steps as I led them inside to their crates, leaned down and latched them in, and gave them each a bone. Standing back up, I took my glasses off, wiped the sweat from my face with my free hand, and slid my glasses back on.

I redid my ponytail as I walked back outside. Perhaps the armadillo had figured out a way to climb out of the pool, now that the threat was gone. Perhaps he had already traveled back to wherever he'd come from, safe and sound. But I soon saw he was still there, swimming his laps around the pool perimeter, periodically trying to claw his way out. His stumpy legs just couldn't get him up over the ledge. I wondered how many laps he could do before he drowned of exhaustion.

I need to help him.

I need someone to help me help him.

Retrieving my phone from my pocket, I called Wilson, who lived a few short blocks away. He was still at work and suggested I call Meredith, who lived about a mile from me. She said Anthony (her newly minted husband of four months) would be home from work any minute, and they'd head over together to see what they could do.

I put my phone back in my pocket and stood there waiting on the scorched concrete pool deck, warily watching the armadillo go round and round the pool, paddling and scrabbling and struggling to stay afloat. As I blinked the tangy sweat from my eyes, it dawned on me that I wasn't going to be able to wait for help to arrive. If that poor creature had any chance of surviving this, I was going to have to try and save him myself.

Looking around, I spotted the recycling bin on the porch. I ran up the steps and dumped out the bottles and cans, then hovered over the side of the pool, dangling the bin in the armadillo's path just under the water. As he approached, I lowered it more, and he swam right in. But when I tried to scoop the bin from the pool, it was too heavy for me (did I mention I had strained a muscle in my back a few weeks prior?); it had taken on too much water. I tipped it to let some of the water out, and the armadillo swam out too.

Dropping the bin on the pool deck with a grunt, I pushed my glasses back up my nose and looked around again. Our detached garage stood behind the pool; maybe something in there would work. I opened the rusty side door and stared into the musty space, waiting for my eyes to adjust to the dimness. I peered at all the junk that had accumulated over the years in there. Nothing seemed suitable for saving a drowning armadillo.

Then my eyes landed on a discarded sign. It had skinny metal legs and advertised a fish fry at the local Catholic church from some years back. Jay's friend, who belonged to the church, had posted it in our front yard since we lived along the main road, but he never retrieved it after the event. I picked it up, thinking I could use it as a sort of ramp, and hurried back to the pool.

Holding the metal legs, I bent down and levered the sign portion into the water in front of the armadillo. Lo and behold, he swam right onto it. My hope expanded. But the surface proved too slick for his feet to get any traction, and he slipped off.

I sat back on my haunches, defeated, my heart thumping hard against my chest, sweat drooling down my spine. The beleaguered armadillo carried on with his vigil of swimming.

Gathering my reserves, I surveyed the yard again and noticed a couple of bricks lying by the patio, over by the chiminea. I wondered if I put a brick on the top pool step, then steered the armadillo to step on the brick, could he then climb out? I ran over and picked up the brick, raced back and placed it on the pool step, then went hunting for something to use to steer him.

A three-foot-long steel rod rested against the side of the house, occasionally used to shut off the main water valve down by the road. It had been left out there forever because it seemed like a convenient place for it to be when needed. I snatched it and hurried back to the pool before the armadillo could complete another lap. As he swam toward me, I stuck my stick in the water and prodded him toward the brick. But once he got near upon it, I realized the distance was still too high for him to hoist himself over the ledge.

I'd need another brick.

I pulled my guide stick out of the water, the armadillo continued swimming, and I sprinted back to the chiminea and grabbed another brick. Coming back to the pool, I placed it on top of the first brick and waited for the armadillo to come around again. When he did, I nudged him toward the bricks with my stick. As soon as his feet hit the top brick, he stepped across it and, just like that, he was out of the pool.

He stood there at the pool's edge, completely still, save the breath heaving in and out of his wet and weary little body. Breathing heavily myself, I slowly leaned over with my hands on my knees and eyed him, glasses sliding down my nose. He eyed me back, then turned and toddled away into the bushes.

I straightened up and realized that I did it. I saved the drowning armadillo.

Just then, my daughter and her husband rushed through the back gate. I had forgotten all about calling them. Anthony, looking around, inquired, "Where's the armadillo?"

Before I could respond, Meredith said, "Mother, you're looking a little disheveled."

I adjusted my glasses and took stock of myself. She was right. My hair was in disarray, having all but abandoned my ponytail, my face felt flushed, and sweat emanated from every pore of my body. I'd have to do more than change my outfit before dinner; I'd have to get a shower and wash my hair too.

Somehow that was okay with me. It no longer seemed to be so much of a bother. And it was then I realized that the person who had called my son, then my daughter to come help was not the same person who had just saved an armadillo from drowning. In a span of ten minutes, I had become someone resourceful, and also resilient. I had forgotten these things about myself in the past seven months.

Maybe I hadn't wanted to remember. Maybe I had wanted to be rescued, was passively waiting for someone—*anyone*—to rescue me from the overwhelming flood of unforeseen circumstances that threatened to drown me.

The day I saved the armadillo was the day I finally believed I could tackle this hard thing looming over me and actually survive it. It was the day I remembered there had been a lot of hard things in my life and I had survived them all. My younger selves had brought me through. Maybe I could channel their resourcefulness and resilience, their grit and determination. Maybe that could give me the courage and the strength to tackle this very hard thing in front of me now.

The day I saved the armadillo was a day of revelation for me. My new day of epiphany.

The armadillo and I, we helped save each other that day.

Chapter 2

The Budweiser Trophy

Thread of Light: Embrace what empowers you

The summer I turned ten years old, I moved with my family to Bossier City, Louisiana. It was the sixth move of my young life. I was born in Arizona, then lived in Florida, Okinawa, Alabama, California, back to Alabama, and then, at ten years old, Louisiana. With my dad being a career air force officer, I didn't know anything different.

In Bossier, we lived in a neighborhood that used to be an old pecan grove. It was named Shady Grove Neighborhood because of the massive pecan trees that surrounded all the houses; we had two in our backyard. Tucked into the middle of the neighborhood was a cozy little library. My mom let me ride my bike there all by myself since it wasn't too far down the tree-lined road from our home. It probably wasn't more than a quarter of a mile, but it felt like a big deal because it was the first time I got to go somewhere all on my own.

On my first visit, the kind librarian showed me around, asked about my interests, and suggested some books for me. I made weekly visits after that, and each time, she would light up when I walked in and ask how I liked reading that week's selection. We would talk about my books, and then she would say something like, "I've been thinking about you this week and wondering what you might want to read next. Let me show you some possibilities."

I discovered the Little House on the Prairie books and imagined myself living a long time ago, way out on the plains, riding a horse instead of a bike. Next came the Trixie Belden series. Trixie lived in the country, rode horses, and was considered a tomboy. I'd not heard this word before. I liked the idea that it was okay for a girl to do the kinds of things boys normally did, like take up space romping around outside, rather than being quiet and small inside. I wanted to be a tomboy too.

That summer I fell in love with reading as I discovered all the places I could go simply by opening a book. Books became my companions, my conversation partners. They nurtured my imagination and fostered a sense of freedom within me.

We only lived in Shady Grove for a year, and I was sad to leave my cozy library and kind librarian behind. But I discovered she had given me a gift that didn't require her presence. I could carry on with my practice of reading wherever I went.

We moved to Scott Air Force Base, just outside Mascoutah, Illinois. It was way out on the plains, but a modern military base in the cornfields felt very different from what I imagined the little house on the prairie to be like—and very different from my experience in Shady Grove, where I rode my bike to the library. The library on the large base was too far away and the roads too busy for me to ride my bike. However, once I started sixth grade at Mascoutah Elementary that fall, I discovered my new school had a library. I found new books to read and explored new adventures through them.

I discovered something else that fall: the base had a recreational sports program for youth, both boys and girls. I was intrigued. Back then, girls didn't play sports like boys did; they took tap dance and ballet lessons. When I was younger, back in California, my mom tried to get me to take ballet, but I didn't want to put on a tutu and slippers and twirl around in circles inside. I wanted to be outside, playing marbles in the dirt and climbing trees in my dungarees. When it came time to get ready for my first lesson, I ran into the front yard and climbed our tree and wouldn't come down. My mom was so mad, but she finally gave in and I didn't have to go to ballet.

The sport that fall at the base youth program was soccer. I'd never played before, but it sounded fun, so I talked my mom into signing me up. And I loved it. Absolutely adored it. I played left wing, where I spent the game running. There were only enough girls to make one team, so we played the boys' teams. It often bothered the boys, but it never bothered us girls at all.

When the season ended, I signed up for the next sport, which was floor hockey, played on an indoor basketball court. This time I was the only girl in the entire league, so they put me on a boys' team. Although I enjoyed it—and even wound up in the penalty box a time or two for unnecessary roughness—I preferred to be outdoors. When the season ended, I was happy to play the next sport, which was softball.

The softball coach tried me at different positions; I liked shortstop and second base best because they saw a lot of action. I wasn't much of a hitter, but if my bat connected with the ball, I usually made it to first base because of my speed. I loved outrunning that ball.

I liked softball better than floor hockey but not as much as soccer. It was the running involved in soccer that really captivated me. So when I got to seventh grade at Mascoutah Junior High and found out there was a track team for girls, I signed up. My favorite races were the sprints, and I usually placed second or third at our meets.

Also that year, I started taking English horseback riding lessons. I thought my Trixie Belden dream was finally coming true. But I came to find out that being up close to a real horse was scary—and getting on top of one was even more terrifying. The grizzled riding instructor who looked like he'd been teaching equestrian students for eons knew just what to do. He put me on an old, stocky quarter horse named Moose, who liked nothing more than to plod along. Moose knew his role with the newbies, and he slowly helped me gain confidence.

With time, I moved on to Tom, a younger bay gelding. He had a bit more spunk than Moose but was also gentle and kind with me. We instantly connected. I learned how to jump with Tom, first in the ring and then on the hunter course. This turned out to be my favorite activity. The riding stable had lots of land and had set up a large course with a number of jumps. I felt like I was gliding through the air on the back of Tom as he masterfully navigated all the hurdles.

Then a new horse came to the stable, and the riding instructor thought she would be a good challenge for me. Katrina was a striking black mare who was headstrong and highstrung. Her demanding way scared me, and I gave in to her. The instructor told me to take control, but I didn't want to fight her. It wasn't in my nature. With Moose and Tom, I had deferred to them and it turned out well because of their easygoing manner. But Katrina was a horse whose personality was contrary to my own, and I wasn't sure we were going to make it as a team.

When we finally got out of the ring and onto the hunter

course, though, we discovered something in common: We both wanted to run like the wind. To feel free. To not be controlled. Whereas Tom would softly canter through the course, Katrina wanted to go at a full-out gallop. That first time out, it took me by surprise. But rather than try and rein her in, I chose to loosen the reins and go with her, settling into her gait. It was exhilarating.

When we returned to the stable, the instructor thought I had lost control, but I shook my head. I knew what I was doing. And I could tell Katrina did too. We finally found a way to move with one another's rhythm without giving up our own. We became a team. We went on to compete together in several shows, winning ribbons in our events.

My family and I lived in Illinois for three years, from the time I was eleven years old until the summer I turned fourteen. It was the longest I remembered ever living anywhere and I had no desire to leave. I had played soccer and softball for three seasons, ran track for two seasons, and rode horses for two years. I didn't want to give any of that up.

Looking back, it feels like those years laid the soil upon which I could grow some interior roots. I would not have called myself adventurous; after all, I was an introverted book nerd. But I had learned that not only my mind but also my body could give me a sense of freedom and power.

And I had made friends over those three years of my adolescence. My own friends. Not just friends of convenience, like you make when you're a child, playing with the neighborhood kids or the children of your parents' friends. These friends were of my own choosing, and I was of their choosing too. Those three years in one place had given me a sense of contented connectedness I didn't want to let go of.

But the longings of a fourteen-year-old girl who had made a

life for herself on the plains of Illinois were not considered when the military said it was time to move.

Our new home was in Carlisle, Pennsylvania, and that fall, feeling lonely and anxious as I began my high school career in a new place, I decided to join the cross-country team. Although I had never run long distances before—the furthest I ran on my junior high track team was the 440, once around the track—I figured if it was running, it would be fun. I wanted to regain that feeling of freedom and power I felt when I ran. Maybe this was a way to connect with the life I left behind.

I was not prepared for the brutal workouts—the long miles we were required to run in practice, interspersed with sprints. I often lagged behind my new teammates. Then, at our first meet, I came in dead last. Sixteenth out of sixteen girls. I was so humiliated—especially because I had run the entire two miles, while I had seen some of the other girls walk some and they still came in ahead of me. I wanted to quit the team.

But something seemed to rise up in my spirit that said, "You can do this." And I wanted to prove to myself that I could.

So I kept trudging along, huffing and puffing at practice, slowly picking up my pace bit by bit. Paying attention to my breathing and my form. Showing up day after sluggish day.

At a meet about a month later, I came in fifth for my team. I began to believe maybe I really *could* do this. I continued to work hard, and the rest of the season I was the fifth runner, rounding out the scoring for our varsity squad.

The following spring, I ran on the track team, where I was the third leg of the mile relay team that set the school record. Four minutes flat. Each of us ran a sixty-second split. I realized that not only could I do this, but with practice and commitment, I could do it well.

My time with this team was short lived, though; that

summer we moved again, this time to Friendly, Maryland, just outside Washington, DC.

When my mom took me to the high school to register for the upcoming school year, I asked the secretary if there was a girls' cross-country team. A big smile came across her face as she exclaimed, "Oh, yes, we have a great cross-country team, both boys and girls, and our very own vice principal is the coach! Hold on a sec, and let me see if he's in. He would love to hear he might have a new runner joining the team."

After she called back to his office, he came out and introduced himself and asked about my running experience. I think he was impressed, especially since I was only a rising sophomore. He gave me the phone number of one of the girls on the team who lived in my new neighborhood and also put me in touch with a group of runners from the team who met weekly to run together. I connected with all of them and soon felt like I belonged to this new community before I even started school.

We officially started practice a week before school started, and I met the rest of the runners, both boys and girls. We practiced together, with the same coach, and I learned that our meets would be together too, although the races were separated by gender. The boys' race was three miles and the girls' was two miles. That first week of practice, I heard some of the girls grumbling about our races being shorter than the boys'. They thought we should run the same distance and complained the disparity was based on an antiquated assumption by male authorities that it would be too much stress on a girl's body to race the longer distance.

"I can't make the rules for what happens at the meets," my new coach responded, "but I *can* make the rules for our practices. And just like in previous years, my boys and girls will practice together, running the same distances with the same hard workouts. No preferential treatment here."

A cheer went up from several of the veteran girls. I liked that the coach saw us as equals, and I was all for being a tomboy, but I wasn't sure I would have what it took to run as hard and as far as the boys. The memory of coming in dead last at my first cross-country meet the previous year niggled at me.

But I need not have worried. My body remembered what it was like to work hard, and by the end of that first week of practice, I had established myself as one of the top five runners on the girls' varsity team.

At practice on the first day of school, I noticed a new face on the boys' team. He was tall and lanky, deeply tanned, with a bushy mop of black curls on his head.

"Who's the new guy?" I asked the girl next to me.

"Oh, he's not new. He's a senior, been on the team several years. His family goes on vacation down to the Outer Banks the last week of August every year, so he gets special permission to miss the first week of practice."

A few weeks later, as I walked across the school parking lot after practice, a car pulled up alongside me. It was the bushy-mop boy in a pale blue Volkswagen Bug.

"Hey, you want a ride home?" he asked, his arm hanging out the car window.

I stopped and looked at him, my eyes squinting against the western sun. "Nah, I'm good. I don't live far from here." I didn't want to be any trouble. My home was about a mile from the school if you took the road. But a swath of woods separated the school from my neighborhood, and walking the trail through the woods cut some time off my commute. Every day I walked to and from school this way.

He looked at me. "You know, we live in the same neighborhood. I practically go right by your house. It's not a problem."

"Oh, well, that's okay. I like the walk." I looked down, scuffing at some loose gravel with my sneaker.

"Really? After running ten miles at practice? I know I'm exhausted. You must be too. Just get in already." And he leaned over and opened the passenger door for me.

Thus began a routine of him giving me a ride home each day after practice. At first, I didn't say much on the short rides to my house. But he asked a lot of questions, me being the new girl and all, and he had a way of inviting me into conversation. We soon became friends, and then I became friends with his friends on the team. There was a camaraderie among all of us as we practiced together and traveled together on the bus to our meets.

One Sunday afternoon in October, about halfway through the season, my doorbell rang. It was the bushy-mop boy. Surprised to see him on my doorstep, I inquired if something was wrong.

He chuckled. "No, nothing's wrong. I just wanted to see if you wanna hang out?"

I was puzzled and looked around to see if any of his friends were lurking about. Not seeing anyone else, I finally asked, "You mean just us? You and me?"

This was uncharted territory, and I tried to get my bearings. Was he suggesting we become more than friends? I didn't dare ask. I'd not thought of him in that way. He really seemed more like a "big brother" type, always watching out for me, giving me rides, introducing me to his friends, cheering me on as I ran. Besides, I had a crush on one of the other seniors on the team, and I thought Bushy Mop might have been pursuing someone himself.

He laughed again. "Yeah, just you and me. Can't two friends hang out together?"

Feeling like he had clarified our standing with one another, I relaxed. "Uh, yeah, I guess so. I mean, sure, why not? You wanna come in?"

We started hanging out together more and more; it was convenient, living in the same neighborhood. His mom invited me to eat dinner with them several times a week. Daily, at six o'clock sharp, Bushy Mop, his three younger sisters, and his parents sat down at the kitchen table to eat. I marveled at this, how they all came together at the end of their day like a cohesive unit. My family never ate together unless it was Thanksgiving or Christmas.

We both became involved with Young Life, a youth ministry that had come to our school. This led to going to church together on Sunday mornings. We often talked about our crushes and gave each other advice. We spent hours playing backgammon and card games; gin rummy was our favorite.

As the school year progressed and winter merged into spring, I found myself on occasion daydreaming about Bushy Mop's lips and what it might feel like to have them brush up against mine. I chastised myself, of course. It was ridiculous. We were friends, good friends, nothing more. But then I'd find myself drifting off again. I began to wonder if maybe he ever imagined the same thing.

Then one night in early June, just a few days before he graduated, Bushy Mop came over to my house to hang out. We sat down on the long green couch in the living room. Shiner, the family dog, was laid out on the orange shag carpet but roused himself to say hello. Bushy Mop seemed nervous and subdued, which unsettled me.

"What's going on?" I asked, studying his face, trying to keep my eyes off his lips.

"I was just wondering," he said, seeming to take forever to continue. "I was wondering," he repeated, pausing again. "Well, I was wondering if you've ever thought about us being more than friends?"

My heart stopped. Then started again with a *thwack* against my chest. It beat in my throat, which made it hard to speak.

Not wanting to appear too eager but also unable to suppress the smile tugging at the corner of my mouth, I whispered, "Have *you?*"

Looking intently into my eyes, he said, "Yes. Yes, I have."

And with that declaration, he leaned in and kissed me softly on the lips.

He had just turned eighteen in May, and I was not yet sixteen years old.

THE CROSS-COUNTRY TEAM felt different my junior year. I missed the first week of practice because I was down in the Outer Banks with Jay and his family. Coach wasn't too happy about that but had given his permission. Then Jay left for college in Florida, and I really pined for him. He not only was my boyfriend; he was my best friend too. Most of my other friends from the team had graduated as well. I was adjusting to a new normal, meeting new friends in my grade. It was awkward.

I had finished the previous year's season as the number-two runner—and the number-one runner had been a senior—so Coach had high expectations for me this season. But I wasn't running up to my potential. He knew I was distracted, and he tried different tactics to motivate me. One day, as our team ran laps around the track, he yelled at me to forget my boyfriend. "He's probably already found another girl down there anyway. I've heard Southern college girls are irresistible. You'll be broken up by Thanksgiving."

I was so humiliated. *Who did I think I was, thinking I could have a college boyfriend?*

Then it just made me mad. At some point, something seemed to rise up in my spirit that said, "You don't have to do this. You don't have to let this man cut you down."

But I love running.

Running had empowered me. I had proven to myself that I could do it—and I did it well. Running had helped me to believe in myself, that I was strong and powerful and capable. But Coach's attitude was tearing it all down. And I didn't have to prove anything to him.

So I finished out the season—as one of the top five runners —and decided I would never run for that coach again. Not wanting to put up with his ridiculing comments, I saw this as my only option.

I didn't say anything to anyone about my decision. But I wrote a poem about it right after the season ended. It was my way of speaking up for myself, even if I was the only one who heard my voice.

Challenge of Yourself

There comes a time
when one must make her own decision.
A time when she must express herself individually
and not by others' evaluations and opinions.
A time when she must disregard
the established pattern of life
and listen to the music she hears—
however far away it may be.

There comes a time
when one must commit herself
to carry out her decision.

A time when she must discipline herself
not to conform to the ways of others.
A time when she must fulfill the responsibility
of letting nothing fade away into emptiness.
And not only listen, but follow the music she hears—
her footsteps setting the beat.

There comes a time
when one must overcome hindrances
so that she may obtain the dreams she imagines.
A time when her prayers will be said
and her prayers will be answered.
The light of truth will be shown.
And not only listen and follow the music she hears—
but whistle the unique tune of her own.

I gave up the sport of running on a school team, but I didn't give up on running. I discovered I loved the freedom of running on my own. No coach to goad me. No time clock to judge me. No competitors breathing down my neck. Just me, myself, and I choosing how far to run, how fast to run, how often to run. It empowered me once again. I fell in love with running just for the sake of it, no strings attached.

I ran on my own the rest of high school and throughout college. When the men's track team at my university hosted a one-mile race open to anyone who wasn't on a collegiate team, I signed up. I won that coed race (six minutes flat) and was presented with a huge trophy constructed with a multitude of Budweiser beer cans. It had to be almost three feet tall and resembled a typical trophy from a bona fide trophy store, the kind of trophy a team might receive for coming in first at a sport. But instead of the pillars between the levels, there were empty Budweiser cans. It turned out Budweiser had co-sponsored the race. I was aghast at the gaudiness of it but so proud of my accomplishment that I kept that trophy out on display. Whenever I looked at it, something seemed to rise up in my spirit that said, "You can do this." And I knew I could.

AFTER DATING long distance for five years, Jay and I married on a rainy day in May, two months shy of my twenty-first birthday. Our wedding was in Ruston, Louisiana, where my parents lived and where I had just finished my junior year at Louisiana Tech University. After our honeymoon, we moved to Chicago, where Jay was in graduate school. I transferred to a nearby university to finish up my undergraduate degree. We lived in a tiny apartment in a high-rise in the heart of the city. I loved being married and finally living together in the same place, but it was a huge transition for me. I was scared to walk the city streets by myself, much less run.

This was around the time I started reading westerns, novels about exploring the American frontier in the 1800s. I had come across a Louis L'Amour novel when Jay and I browsed a secondhand bookshop, and I got hooked. Although the plots were repetitive, I enjoyed their themes of freedom and autonomy and imagined myself traversing the great outdoors on horseback rather than walking the concrete streets of Chicago. L'Amour's series on the Sackett family was my favorite. The brothers were loyal to one another while always doing the right thing for others. Reading those books gave me a sense of agency in my spirit when other parts of my life seemed constricting.

Eventually I found a running partner through the church we attended, and she and I began running together most mornings before work. She lived about five blocks from me and only two blocks from the lakefront, so when the weather was warmer, we often ran there. It felt liberating to run next to that great expanse of water. But during the frigid winters, when the artic wind blew hard, we stuck to the streets.

I was not cut out for city living or for long, dismal winters with little sunshine for months, so I was elated when, after three years in Chicago, Jay was offered a position in Florida. It felt so good to run among greenery, up and down spacious residential streets rather than in and out of crowds and around commercial buildings. I didn't even mind the sweltering summer months. And although a running partner had been an essential part of my routine in Chicago, I loved the freedom of running alone in Florida. Those first few years, I found myself wanting to go further and faster on my runs, often running five miles or more at a seven-minute-mile pace.

I ran during my first pregnancy and then while pushing Wilson in his stroller once I became a mom. When Meredith came along, I upgraded to a Baby Jogger double stroller so I could keep running. Once April was born, I hired a babysitter several times a week when I couldn't get my run in otherwise.

My love affair with running lasted thirty years—until my right knee finally gave out. I went to the orthopedist, hoping he could fix it, but instead he advised me to stop running. "If you don't stop running now," he warned, "in twenty years you won't be able to walk."

It was the summer I turned forty-two. Over the last three decades, running had become synonymous with who I was. It was my identity. I was a runner. Running had given me so much. It helped me believe in myself, that I was strong and powerful and capable. And running always found a way to settle my unsettledness, recalibrate my inner compass, and remind me that I can do whatever hard thing was still in front of me to do.

I felt like I had lost all of that.

I felt untethered.

So I turned to reading again. And since it was summer, I started with beach reads. At first, they felt like fluff and a good way to escape my non-runner reality. But then I discovered authors who wove intriguing stories of depth, drama, and charm while dealing with real-life issues—authors like Jennifer Weiner and Marian Keyes. I loved how their main characters became the heroines of their own stories. They possessed courage and wisdom and grit. They were resourceful and creative and tenacious. The more I read, the more it occurred to me that I possessed some of those same qualities myself. I realized there's more to who I am than my identity as a runner. Reading those novels helped me claim a more holistic vision of myself.

I could do this. I could live without running.

Even though I no longer could run (and the Budweiser trophy had long since met its demise), I could still hear the echo of those long-ago words: "You can do this." And within that echo: "You don't have to do this."

You can do the hard things that will lead to your empowerment. You don't have to do the things that will lead to your diminishment.

Chapter 3

The Hospital Letter

Thread of Light: Find your voice and trust yourself to use it

"Honey, are you in labor?" a grandmotherly-looking woman asked me. I was sitting in a small, cramped waiting room, every chair filled with these grandmotherly and grandfatherly types, in the Labor and Delivery ward of our local hospital. Every time I had a contraction, a little more amniotic fluid seeped out. I felt my face grow warm when her question brought everyone's attention to my situation.

Jay and I had just been to my OB's office, where, to everyone's surprise, my water broke. My doctor had sent me to the hospital, just around the corner, saying he would come over once I got settled. Jay dropped me off at the hospital entrance, then went to park the car. When I checked in at the nurses' station, the clerk said there were no clean rooms and directed me to wait in the visitors' waiting room.

I had stared at her. Surely, she didn't understand. I was in labor. In my mind, this baby was going to be born in mere hours, just like my first child was.

I hesitated, then reiterated, "But . . . *I'm in labor.* My water just broke a little bit ago."

The clerk stared back with an assessing eye. "Well, you're still able to talk, so you can't be too far along. It'll only be a few minutes. We've got housekeeping working on the empty rooms now."

"Um . . . okay," I heard myself squeak, resigned, as I turned and walked to the waiting room.

That was where I was sitting when Jay showed up, poking his head in the doorway.

He looked perplexed. "What are you doing in here?" he asked.

"They told me to wait here while they clean a room."

All the heads of all the soon-to-be grandmothers and grandfathers turned to me in fascination.

"That's ridiculous!" he cried. "Did you tell them you're in labor? That your water broke?"

"Yes! Yes, I did. It didn't seem to make a difference. They basically said if I can talk, then I can wait."

Jay harrumphed as he made his way past everyone and sat down in the chair next to me that I had saved for him.

We waited and waited.

The contractions came closer together, and I wondered if I should have been more insistent with the clerk. My labor with Wilson was less than three hours, and I could still talk when it came time to push. *Should I have told her that? Why didn't I stand up for myself?*

After waiting some more, Jay declared, "This is absurd! I'm going to see what's taking so long. You should be in a room by now."

I nodded.

After a few minutes, he came back and said, "Come on. I talked them into letting you wait in the exam room until one of the regular rooms is available."

I followed him back to the nurses' station, and one of the nurses escorted us to the exam room. She looked put out as she instructed me, "You can wait in here on the gurney. No need to change into a gown yet. We'll wait until we get you in a room. Then we'll properly admit you and examine you to see how far along you are."

You're leaving without even checking me? Really?

I stared at her retreating back.

Jay grumbled something under his breath, sat down in the chair next to my gurney, then turned his attention to me. "How close are your contractions? Here, let's time them."

They were two minutes apart and increasingly painful, my huge belly tightening as I felt the familiar cramping deep within. I drew into myself. After ten to fifteen minutes of timing the contractions and no one returning to check on me, Jay stood up and said, "That's it! That's enough of this nonsense. I'm going to tell them you feel like you need to push. That will get them in here."

"But I don't feel like I need to push," I protested. "Just tell them how close the contractions are and how long they're lasting."

"Nope, I'm going to tell them you have to push." And he left just as another wave of cramping came upon me.

Next thing I knew, a nurse ran in and got me out of my clothes in a flurry so she could check me. Eight centimeters. I could see the surprise and worry etched across her face. "We need to get you in a room—stat." She got on the intercom and called the nurses' station, and two other nurses came in, bustling around me. The three of them rolled my gurney out of the room and down the hall.

Out of nowhere, it seemed, a freight train rumbled full throttle down the track of my insides, and I had an urgent, primal need to expel it. I groaned loudly as the waves of pain came, one on top of another. "I think . . . I think the baby's coming . . . I can feel . . . *the baby's coming!*"

The nurse was stern. "*Don't* push! Whatever you do, *don't* push! We need to get you in a room before you deliver."

She told one of the nurses to put her hand between my legs and apply pressure if needed to keep the baby in. The nurse did as she was told, then informed us all, "The head has crowned!"

The third nurse got right in my face and said, "You need to pant to stop the pushing. Follow my lead." And she started huffing and puffing—*huff, huff, poof*—her mouth not two inches from mine as the nurses picked up their pace moving the gurney down the hall.

I tried huffing and puffing, but it turned into loud, mournful wails as I rode the waves. I groaned, "I can't hold it in . . . I can't . . . I can't!"

"Yes, you can! Yes, you can!" panted the nurse in my face. *Huff, huff, poof. Huff, huff, poof.*

They swept me and my gurney into a room at the end of the hall while shooing out a startled housekeeper with her mop. I could hear the overhead speaker: "Resident, stat! L and D! Resident, stat, Labor and Delivery." And then, miraculously it seemed, a medical resident appeared and took charge.

She said, "It's time to push your baby out. Let's do it."

I let my body do what it knew to do, and the freight train finally lost its steam and chugged on out of me.

I collapsed like a rag doll. There was a prolonged hush in the room as the others caught up with themselves. Then the resident laid my newborn child—who hadn't made a sound, not even a whimper—on top of me.

Finally, belatedly, Jay exclaimed, "It's a girl! We have a baby girl!"

About an hour had lapsed since I showed up at the nurses' station. If it hadn't been for Jay's advocacy, I probably would have delivered Meredith in the waiting room.

LESS THAN A WEEK LATER, we were back at the same hospital, this time in the ER because Meredith, at six days old, was running a fever of 102. I was beside myself. She was so tiny, lying there on the big gurney in the small exam cubicle. They tried to start an IV, and she screamed that newborn wail, her face red and scrunched up. They wouldn't let me hold her. Tears streamed down my face as I looked on over their shoulders, imagining all the horrible things that might be wrong with my baby. My milk let down. A nurse suggested I wait in the waiting room, but I said no. I would stay right where I was. Even Jay thought we should go to the waiting room, touching my elbow to steer me that way. But I pulled away.

"I'm not leaving my baby," I said. "I'm staying right here."

They said they needed to do some tests to determine why she had a fever, that one-week-old babies don't have fevers for no reason. So they drew blood from her heel, which drew more screams. And more tears down my face. They took off her diaper and waited for her to pee so they could collect some urine. They did a chest x-ray and a spinal tap. Jay sat down in the one chair in the exam area after offering it to me, but I wouldn't leave her side. I could tell they thought I was in the way. I thought they were absurd. I was her *mother*, for God's sake.

My breasts were filling up; I needed to nurse. Finally, when they were done with the first round of poking and prodding and she kept crying, I said, "She's hungry. I need to feed her."

Finally, they looked at me like I was someone other than a nuisance. Finally, they handed me my baby, and when I lifted up my shirt and unfastened my nursing bra, Meredith latched on furiously, trying to gulp down my milk. Tears kept sliding down my face as I held her close, rocking back and forth, trying to calm us both down.

The tests revealed Meredith had a urinary tract infection. I blamed myself. It must have been because I didn't take proper care when changing her diaper. I wasn't used to baby girls. But they said no, it wasn't anything I did, that newborns don't get UTIs like that. There was something else going on that caused it. They wanted to admit her to the hospital so they could start her on IV antibiotics and do more tests to figure out the cause.

Even though she was a newborn, she wasn't admitted to the neonatal intensive care unit because she had already gone home after her birth. The NICU, I found out, was only for babies who had never left the hospital after being born. So we went to the pediatric unit, and this turned out to be a good thing. Because Meredith was a breastfed baby, she was given a private room, which also had a private bathroom, and the chair in the room could unfold into a single bed. I stayed with her around the clock for the five days she was there.

This met with a lot of pushback from everyone. The doctors, nurses, and aides said I should take a break, go home, get some rest. Even Jay tried to get me out of the hospital. I finally gave in one evening and went to dinner with him at a nearby restaurant. But I couldn't relax. All I could think about was tiny newborn Meredith lying all by herself in that cavernous crib in that sterile hospital room. I finally told Jay to get our food boxed up to take with us. I was ready to head back.

That was the one and only time I left Meredith during her hospital stay. I was unwavering in my conviction that I knew what was best for her, that being by her side was best.

Some might call it a mother's intuition, that sense that you know what you should do for the well-being of your child, even if others minimize or dismiss your concerns. Whether or not it is intuition, I know that it felt much more natural for me to advocate for my child than it did to advocate for myself only a week earlier.

At first, it didn't seem to matter. All I felt was relief and gratitude that all had ended well, both with Meredith's birth and with her hospital stay. I was so relieved there were no complications with the birth despite my unconventional labor and delivery. And I was grateful the doctors figured out the reason Meredith had an UTI. They said her ureters (the tubes that connect the kidneys to the bladder) were allowing urine to back up from the bladder to the kidneys, causing infection. We were told this condition is not uncommon in newborns and that over the next one to two years, Meredith's ureters would hopefully correct themselves as she grew. She would need to be monitored to make sure that was happening, and in the meantime, she would need to stay on a low dose of oral antibiotics to prevent any more infections.

Once we were home from the hospital, we settled into the typical newborn-in-the-house rhythm of sleepless nights, endless feedings, laundry, and dirty dishes. We also had to be vigilant about keeping two-year-old Wilson from walloping his new baby sister (which he had tried to do because he "wanted to see if she was real").

In the midst of all this, I started reliving Meredith's birth experience. I couldn't stop thinking about it. My humiliation waiting in the visitors' waiting room, leaking amniotic fluid while others looked on in fascination. Feeling like I was center stage at a circus show. My guilt for not letting the staff know I had a history of fast labor. My guilt for not insisting they check me when I first got there, then again when they left me in the exam room. The trauma of trying to hold the baby back, even after her head had crowned. The chaos of being in active labor, careening toward delivery, while traversing the hallway on a gurney. The disappointment that a stranger delivered my baby rather than my familiar doctor. The deep, aching sadness that all of that might have been prevented if I had just spoken up. If I had just stood up for myself and insisted, I might have had a completely different experience. I might have been engaging in a cherished memory rather than reliving a roller-coaster ride that ran off the rails.

I blamed myself. And I berated myself for continuing to relive it. There was no use crying over spilt milk, as the saying goes. But I couldn't help myself as I kept rehashing the scenes in my mind.

As I processed my experience of Meredith's birth, images of her subsequent hospital stay came to mind. My refusal to wait in the waiting room. My insistence that I would stay with my baby. My conviction that I knew what was best for her. As those images came into focus, mingling with all the emotions from Meredith's birth, something shifted for me. I came to an awareness that what happened with Meredith's birth was not my fault.

I should not have had to speak up, to stand up, to insist. The hospital staff should have asked me questions to assess my specific situation and then given me appropriate attention. They never asked how close together my contractions were. They never hooked me up to a monitor so they could check Meredith's well-being in utero. Instead, they made assumptions. Judgments. Which is how I ended up hanging on to a runaway roller coaster rather than reclining in a pontoon boat floating at the river's edge.

No one should have to go through that. It made me wonder how many other women had experienced something similar. It occurred to me that women may be going through that even as I was thinking about it.

Somebody should say something. Somebody should speak up and let the hospital administration know this wasn't the way to treat laboring women.

That's when I heard this voice within my spirit: *What about you?*

What *about* me? What could *I* do? No one would listen to me. No one paid attention to me during the birth experience, so why would they pay attention to me now?

But then those same images from Meredith's hospital stay popped into my head again. My refusal to wait in the waiting room. My insistence that I would stay with my baby, day and night. My conviction that I knew what was best for her.

How was it that I could advocate for Meredith but not for myself?

As I wrestled with that question, I realized that during Meredith's hospital stay, I was in a position of strength as her mother. From that position, I was able to speak up for my vulnerable child. This led me to recognize how vulnerable I had been as a laboring woman about to give birth and how being in that position made it hard to speak up for myself.

Thinking of this made me want to shower myself with compassion. This led to me feeling compassion for all those laboring women who show up at the hospital as their most vulnerable selves. Who, like me, might not be able to speak up for themselves when the staff minimizes or dismisses their concerns.

Who was going to advocate for them?

As I sat there with those thoughts swirling around me, an idea came. I could write a letter. A letter to the hospital administration—the CEO, the director of nursing, and the department that says they represent the patients—letting them all know what happened. It might help other women in similar situations. It might help the Labor and Delivery staff adopt new protocols and treat their patients with more dignity, respect, and compassion. I felt like writing the letter would help me feel like I finally spoke up for myself, even if it was after the fact.

So that's what I did. I wrote a letter and sent it to the CEO, the director of nursing, and the patient representative department. I told them all about my birthing experience with their staff. *All* the details. It probably was too much information. Oh well. They could deal with it.

About a week later, I received a letter in response:

> Thank you for taking the time to let us know about your recent experience. We are committed to continued improvement of our facility and services, and sincerely appreciate your comments. It is because of patients like you who care enough to let us know about your experience that we can identify problems and correct them. We assure you that all comments are investigated thoroughly and appropriate action is taken.

I don't know if that response was just a bunch of hot air or if anything really changed there. But what I do know is that writing that letter changed *me*.

The stark contrast of standing up for Meredith right on the heels of *not* standing up for myself showed me that I had what I needed within me not only to advocate for others, but also to advocate for myself.

This became a pattern that continued over the years of

raising my children. I advocated for them with their doctors, their teachers, their coaches, and yes, even with their father. And the more practice I had speaking up on their behalf, the more confidence I gained to speak up for myself when I needed to. Advocating for my children helped me find my voice and trust myself to use it on my own behalf.

Chapter 4

My Body Knew

Thread of Light: Claim the courage to seek the truth

I was diagnosed with depression the summer I turned thirty-six, the same year we rebuilt our old, dilapidated home. I didn't realize it at the time, but rebuilding our house was a fitting metaphor for the experience of rebuilding myself.

Jay and I had bought the home six years prior; Wilson had just turned three and Meredith was one. A quaint home built in the early 1900s, it was definitely a fixer-upper, but we didn't mind. We loved that it had a beautiful view of the river and was centrally located in the small, historic district of our coastal town. With the renovations we hoped to eventually do, my plan was for this house to be the home where my children grew up, where they would come home to visit when they were grown, where they would bring their future children one day. I advocated for this on behalf of our children. I told Jay I did not want our kids growing up like I did, moving every year or two, feeling uprooted and rootless. I wanted them to be raised in the same house in the same neighborhood in the same town so they would always feel like they had a home, like they belonged. I wanted this for myself too. I wanted to feel rooted. I longed to live out my adult life in the same house, the same neighborhood, the same town.

Our ninety-year-old home was cobbled together from what was originally a small barn that housed the horse and carriage for the two stately homes on either side of it. There had been three to four shoddy additions over the decades, which left the home with no architectural integrity. What once had been a barn became a cottage, then a bungalow, then a two-story family home struggling to resemble the dignified homes surrounding it. It was like our home had been given some hand-me-down clothes, and none of them ever quite fit.

In this old home, uninvited guests often showed up. Like the birds who flew out from behind the stove; the river rats (think Templeton from *Charlotte's Web*) who ran through the furnace room and inside the uninsulated walls; and the little white mice that poked their pink noses out from the cabinet underneath the kitchen sink. In the early years, at night, when we were all asleep, one or more of these creatures—we never quite knew which—ventured out of hiding and chewed the nipples off April's baby bottles that I'd been too tired to rinse out before falling asleep, trying to get to the residual milk inside.

We always knew we would renovate once we had the resources to do so, but when that time came, our contractor told us what the home really needed was a complete rebuild.

So we deconstructed before we reconstructed. We sifted and sorted, deciding what was worth saving and what should be discarded. We hired a salvage company that specialized in removing vintage bones from old homes. They pried up, board by board, the heart pine flooring that had been in the first addition, then the one-inch oak flooring that had been in the bedrooms of the second-story addition. The floors we walked upon in our old home would become the same floors we walked upon in our new home.

They dismantled the solid cypress paneling that had been the original walls, which would become the ceilings of our new front and back porches. They lifted out the small, square-shaped bathtub where I bathed my three children as toddlers; we would carry those memories with us as we used this tub in its new space. They uncovered one of the structural beams from the original barn so we could repurpose it as a mantle over our new fireplace. We gathered up all these fragments, these historical treasures, and integrated them into our new home.

We loosely kept the footprint of the house. After all, it was being rebuilt in the exact same place the old house had been. We knew which rooms worked and which ones needed modification in size or location. We knew the rooms that welcomed the early morning light and the ones that needed protection from the afternoon heat. Six years of our family's memories were embedded in this home, and we wanted our new home to have the same feel without all the unnecessary baggage.

Initially, our children were not on board with the project. This was the only home Wilson and Meredith, nine and seven years old, remembered and the only home five-year-old April had ever lived in. They didn't want something new. For them, family was synonymous with the home in which that family resided. What would happen to their family if their house was no longer the same? They did not have the life experience to realize we carry family with us—the good, the bad, the ugly—regardless of where we live. Those memories live deep in our hearts, our muscles, our bones.

MY DIAGNOSIS of depression came on the heels of trying to hold it all together for years. I had constructed a nice, orderly life: college, marriage, career, children. I even spaced the births of my three children in an orderly manner. First one child; then twenty-three months later, a second child; then twenty-three months later, a third child.

But that is when it all started to fall apart. *I* started to fall apart. I assumed it had to do with the chaos that ensued when I no longer had enough hands to hold the hands of my three children. Disorder had invaded my orderly life.

Right after April was born, I began having headaches. Too busy with a newborn, a toddler, and a preschooler, I put up with my aching head for six months until, worried I had a brain tumor, I made an appointment with my family doctor. He asked me to fill out a questionnaire, and once he reviewed my responses, he turned to me and proclaimed, "You are overwhelmed with the care of your three little children. You need to take some time for yourself. Take care of yourself. Your stress is causing your headaches."

I guess I needed his permission because I listened to his advice. I paid attention to caring for myself while caring for the children. I rested when they did, instead of trying to get one more thing done. I sat down to eat with them when I fed them, rather than just grabbing a bite while cleaning up. I hired a babysitter so I could exercise when my husband wasn't around. Eventually, the headaches went away.

The following year, I started having lower abdominal pain. After seeing my family doctor, he referred me to a urologist, who determined my pain was caused by bladder spasms. I underwent extensive testing, then a referral to my gynecologist, but they couldn't find a reason why. My bladder was completely healthy, just spasming painfully. After trying different medications over several months, none of which seemed to make a difference, the spasms eventually went away on their own.

Around the time April turned two, an intense upper abdominal pain set in. After several tests, it was determined my gallbladder was spasming, and it was recommended it be removed. The general surgeon who performed the surgery happened to be a friend from church, whose name was Peter. At the surgical post-op visit, he expressed concern that my gallbladder had no pathology. In other words, it was healthy, which meant there was no identifiable cause for the spasming. I didn't care, though, because the pain was gone.

Early the next year, I made an appointment with my gynecologist because of ongoing heavy, lengthy, and painful menstrual periods, a chronic condition that had progressively worsened since April's birth. The gynecologist recommended several options, including a hysterectomy. I chose the surgery, which was supposed to be a minor thing; rather than cutting open my abdomen, my GYN would go in vaginally to retrieve the uterus. My surgery was scheduled for the Wednesday before Easter. I'd be home the next day and recovered by Sunday to celebrate the holiday with my family.

After the surgery, I woke up on a gurney in the post-op recovery unit. My gynecologist came by and told me all had gone well. Then he added that, in addition to removing my uterus, he also removed one of my ovaries because he found a cyst on it.

I nodded and, heavy lidded from the anesthesia, drifted back to sleep.

The next time I woke up—several hours later—Jay was hovering over me, saying goodbye. Not the kind of goodbye like

"See you later." More the kind of goodbye like "I'm not sure when I'll see you again."

Where am I going?

I tried to ask, formed the words in my head, could taste them in my mouth, but nothing came out when I tried to speak. Something wasn't right. Actually, something felt very wrong with my entire body, but I couldn't make any words come out to explain, to ask for help, to say anything at all to my husband. He looked so worried.

Where am I going?

Just then, someone started rolling my gurney out the door of the post-op recovery unit, down the hall, and into another room, where they stopped right under some very bright lights.

Where am I? And why can't someone give me something to make me feel better?

All of a sudden, Peter—my general surgeon friend from church—came into view.

What is he doing here?

He leaned in and said, "I'm going to take good care of you, Melynne. We all are." That's when I noticed how many people were in the room, all moving around purposefully.

Peter continued, "We think you're bleeding internally. And from your vital signs, you've probably lost a significant amount of blood. We need to open you up and find where it's coming from. We'll be making an incision from your belly button down to your pubic area so we can see what's going on. This is beyond the scope of your GYN, so I was called in."

Then my lights went out.

When I woke up, I was lying in a bed in the surgical intensive care unit with a ton of tubes attached to my body. I was told a small blood vessel had not been cauterized when my GYN cut out my ovary; that was the source of the bleeding. I also was told I had lost more than half my body's blood and ordinarily would have been given a blood transfusion. But because it was the years following the AIDS epidemic, there were still concerns about the virus showing up in donated blood. Since I lost my blood internally, the thinking was that my body could reabsorb the lost blood. This way, I could avoid the risk of a tainted blood transfusion.

That all seemed fine to me, except I came to quickly find out it takes a good, long while to reabsorb all that wayward blood. In the meantime, I had to deal with the side effects of not enough blood circulating through my body. The unrelenting, round-the-clock headaches were the worst. Then there was the all-consuming fatigue and weakness. A body needs blood to work. I looked like a ghost of myself, my skin colorless from lack of blood.

Jay didn't want the children to visit me in the hospital because he thought they would be frightened by how I looked. But after several days, seven-year-old Wilson decided I must be dead since I didn't come home when I said I would. Even at such a young age, he had a discerning spirit and often was attuned to the various emotions swirling around us. I pleaded with Jay to let Wilson come see me, and he finally relented. Wilson was so relieved to see me in the living flesh—even if it was a ghostly flesh—that he climbed right up on my bed and snuggled in for a good, long hug. He knew what he needed. And maybe he knew what I needed too. His engaging presence and warm embrace helped me remember my identity extended beyond the one-dimensional status of a hospital patient.

I was in the hospital more than a week. I completely missed Easter with my children. Once I was discharged, it took several long months to fully recover. Jay managed it all, hiring a young woman to take care of the kids, cook meals, and keep the house tidy while I convalesced. It hadn't occurred to me I wouldn't be able to do those things when I went home.

As with my gallbladder, the post-operative pathology report from my hysterectomy declared my uterus healthy. There was no apparent cause for the extreme cramping that characterized my menstrual pain. It made me wonder if my uterus had been spasming like my other organs had. It reminded me of my last two pregnancies, when I was diagnosed with an irritable uterus. With each pregnancy, early in my eighth month of gestation, I had gone into what we thought was premature labor. But because my cervix didn't dilate with the contractions, this condition wasn't considered true premature labor. An irritable uterus was one that spasmed for no apparent reason.

Life slowly returned to normal as I began to feel like myself again. Meredith started kindergarten that fall and had already fallen in love with reading. A girl after my own heart. I remember sitting with her one evening at bedtime, listening to her sound out the words on the page of her primer, when I became aware of discomfort in my jaw. I rubbed the area and opened and closed my mouth several times. It felt like a muscle was too tight.

It went downhill from there. When I saw my doctor, he diagnosed my condition as temporomandibular joint disorder (TMJ), which is muscular in nature. He recommended exercises to help my jaw relax, to help *me* relax, he said. Apparently, clenching my jaw had become routine and I was totally unaware of it. He also recommended I wear a mouth guard at night to help with the clenching and possible teeth grinding.

But when I began to experience lightning-like flashes of pain down the side of my face, he referred me to a neurologist, who diagnosed my condition as trigeminal neuralgia (TN), which is nerve related. The neurologist said TN pain follows the course of the trigeminal nerve, which originates in the brain stem and runs up and around the ear and down the cheek.

Initially, medications were effective in my treatment, but eventually the pain couldn't be suppressed. Although at times it occurred spontaneously, it was more likely to be triggered by everyday activities, such as chewing, brushing my teeth, smiling, laughing, and sometimes even talking.

By the next summer, the pain had become so debilitating that the neurologist suggested surgery. There were no neurosurgeons in my area who did this procedure, so Jay and I drove two hours to the teaching hospital affiliated with the University of Florida in Gainesville. At the presurgical consultation, the surgeon explained the cause of TN was thought to be from an artery pressing on the nerve close to the point where the nerve exits the brain. He would perform a craniotomy (drill a hole in my skull), move the artery away from the nerve, and use a permanent clip to keep it out of the way.

Although it was technically considered brain surgery, it sounded straightforward, a possible means to eliminate the unbearable pain. We scheduled the surgery for September, once school was back in session and four-year-old April would start her prekindergarten year.

Jay's mother came down from Virginia to stay with the children while we traveled to Gainesville for the surgery. When the surgeon went in, he found there was *not* an artery pressing on the nerve, but rather a vein, which he moved away from the nerve. He expressed some concern that because a vein is much smaller than an artery, presumably it would not put as much pressure on the nerve, so he wasn't sure if that had been the cause of my pain. He said we would have to "wait and see" if the surgery helped.

My pain subsided over the following months, and I was able to enjoy all the festivities of Thanksgiving and Christmas.

But then, in February, seemingly out of nowhere, the pain returned with intensity when I bit into a plum.

I was devastated.

Jay suggested we make an appointment with the neurosurgeon to discuss further options. On a Friday morning, we drove the two hours back to Gainesville.

I CAN STILL VISUALIZE the small exam room where we waited for the surgeon. It wasn't long after he entered the room that Jay blurted out, "Do you think Melynne's nerve pain could stem from mental issues? That maybe all this could be caused by depression?"

I stared alarmingly at my husband. I couldn't compute that his mouth had spoken those words. I was dumbfounded and offended that he could *think*, much less *suggest*, I had a mental problem.

I remember the sound of my heart thumping hard in my ears, the walls of the room beginning to close in, as the surgeon responded, "Well, yes, that could be a possibility. This type of pain can, at times, be psychoneurogenic in nature. And it was something I considered when you all came for the presurgical consultation."

Was he suggesting my pain was not real? How outrageous!

He kept talking like I was no longer there, seated right across from him. "I noticed at that time that Melynne had a flat affect, which, of course, is one of the signs of depression."

I wanted to scream, *I had a flat affect because it hurt to move my face!*

But I said nothing.

He went on to say more— "There were several other red flags . . ."—but I lost focus, the roar in my ears drowning out his monotonous tone. Eventually, I heard him say, "But overall, I thought it would be prudent to proceed with the surgery." He said it like he talked about these kinds of earth-shattering things every day.

It felt like all the oxygen had been whisked out of the room. I could no longer breathe and could feel myself dwindling like a balloon that shrivels with no air, until it seemed neither my husband nor the surgeon were aware of my presence.

The surgeon droned on as he spoke directly to Jay. "We can always go back in. Sometimes there is the possibility that the clip we placed to hold the vessel away from the nerve has slipped. Sometimes that happens. But since you have brought up the question of a psychosomatic etiology, I think it seems wise to explore that avenue before we consider another surgery."

The surgeon finally glanced over at me before finishing with, "I can put in a referral for a psychiatrist, if you like."

By this time, my jaw was dropping. I could not believe how this appointment had unfolded—no *flat affect* anymore. The rest of my body was taut, tense, firing on all cylinders, readying itself for fight or flight. I'd always preferred flight, and I wanted to save my reserves to fight this out with Jay in private, so I managed to rasp out, "No, no, thank you," as I gathered my purse to leave.

Jay added, "We'll look into finding someone closer to home. We'll be back in touch if we need to pursue this with you."

We walked through the halls of the hospital in silence. Walked out the door and across the campus to the parking garage in silence.

But as soon as we got into the car, I laid into him. "What were you *thinking?* I cannot believe you brought up the ridiculous idea that I might be depressed, that all of this might be from depression. *Are you out of your mind?*"

He sat there, taking it in, like he expected this reaction from me. Finally, he responded, "Just hear me out. I've been carrying this a long time, and I just need you to hear me out."

He told me about a conversation he had with our friend, Peter, the same Peter who was the general surgeon who saved me when I almost bled to death. The same Peter who removed my gallbladder. Over these few years, he and Jay had become good friends. Apparently, Peter had approached my husband just before my brain surgery to tell him he thought I had depression and that in his opinion, both as a friend and a physician, depression was causing all my pain. He advised Jay to talk me out of the surgery. But Jay wasn't convinced, so he kept this news to himself. Now that the pain had recurred, Jay felt he should confront me about it and explore the possibility.

I sat there in stunned silence, fuming. Now I also was furious with Peter. The audacity of assuming he knew me well enough to suggest such a thing. I was beside myself with both of them, talking about me behind my back. I seethed the entire two-hour drive home.

As soon as we pulled into our gravel driveway and Jay turned off the ignition, I opened my door to get out, to get away. But he put his hand on my arm and said, "Melynne, wait. I want you to at least think about it. Think about seeing someone. I don't see what harm it could do to talk about the possibility."

My jaw was set in a line so tight, it made my face hurt. Staring straight ahead, I spit out between clenched teeth, "I can't believe you don't think my pain is real."

"But I do!" he cried. "I do believe it's real. Just because it comes from a psychological source rather than an anatomical or physiological source doesn't mean it's not real. It can be a real, physical manifestation with a different root cause."

Without responding, I got out of the car in a huff and slammed the door behind me.

I stewed over it all weekend, vacillating between indignation (how *dare* they suggest such a thing!) to embarrassment (what have I done to give Peter the impression there's something wrong with me?) to shame (*is* there something wrong with me?). It felt way too uncomfortable to linger with this feeling of shame, this feeling that there was something fundamentally wrong with me at my core, that my mind shuffled back to indignation, which felt like a much safer place to be.

And so indignation propelled me forward with a plan. *Sure,* went the monologue in my head, *I'll go see somebody. I'll appease my husband and his friend. Just so I can prove them wrong.*

I was adamant I be the one to choose the mental health professional I would go see. But who? I refused to even consider seeing a psychiatrist. I didn't want someone taking one look at me and slapping me with a drearisome diagnosis and some so-called happy pills. And I *loathed* the idea of seeing someone who called themselves a therapist. Although I had never been to therapy, my idea of what happened there felt too . . . too . . . I don't know . . . too touchy-feely with my emotions . . . too invasive of my private thoughts.

But who could I see that wouldn't be completely scary?

I remembered hearing about a counselor at our church. He had been a church pastor in the past but went back to school for an advanced counseling degree. Now counseling was his full-time job. I think they called him a pastoral counselor. I really had no idea how—or if—he was any different from a therapist, but he sounded less threatening, so I made an appointment.

After introductions, the counselor inquired, "So, what brings you here today?"

Anticipating this kind of question, I had rehearsed my

response. I confidently replied, "So, my husband is having a hard time dealing with my medical problems, and I need some advice on how to help him come to terms with accepting this reality."

When I reflect back on what I said, I can only imagine how hard it must have been for the counselor to keep a straight face. But I was serious. And to his credit, he followed my lead. He knew I was in denial and that it would do no good for him to point that out. Denial, writes author Terry Tempest Williams, "protects us from the potency of a truth we cannot yet bear to accept. . . . [It] cleverly constructs walls around us to keep us safe."[1]

The counselor knew the only way to deconstruct those walls was to help me discover another way to feel safe. So we spent the next six months talking about all kinds of things completely unrelated to what made me feel unsafe. I felt like the counselor really listened to me. He respected me. He didn't draw hasty assumptions about who I was or what my pain was about. Eventually, I felt safe enough to consider bringing up the real reason I had sought him out.

It was sometime late that summer—the same summer we rebuilt our home—that I told him about my husband and his friend thinking I had depression, how they thought depression caused my physical pain. That Jay had wanted me to see a counselor "to explore the possibility."

I asked him what he thought about that. And like any counselor worth their salt, he turned the question around.

"What do *you* think about that?" he inquired.

Frustrated with his tactics, I replied, "I don't know!"

He waited.

I waited, seeing if I could wait him out.

Finally, exasperated, I said, "I'm thinking maybe I don't even know what depression is. Isn't it about feeling sad all the time? I don't think I feel sad all the time." I took a breath, then added, "Actually, I don't think I *feel* much of anything."

I waited for him to respond, but he just said, "Say more about that."

Ugh. What am I paying him for if I'm the one who has to figure everything out for myself?

He waited, and his calm presence helped me settle myself. I thought about it. "Well, like when you ask how I feel about something and I respond by telling you what I *think* about it, not what I *feel* about it. It's because I don't know if I feel anything. Life just kind of feels flat."

I paused.

That's not what I meant.

He waited.

"I mean, I can see that life's not flat. I can see my kids having fun, laughing and playing. And I want to have fun too, have fun with them. But it's like that feeling is somewhere outside of me. I want to capture it, call it my own feeling, but it keeps flitting away, somewhere beyond my reach."

I sighed.

This is hard.

I tried again. "Maybe it's not that *life* feels flat, but that *I* feel flat, because I can't figure out how to feel what I want to feel."

I sat there, depleted.

Then, in a small voice, I finished, "It all makes me rather sad."

My counselor nodded, and we sat together in the silence of that truth.

That is how my denial began to ebb away and I let myself consider that perhaps I might have a touch of depression.

∼

As I CONTINUED THERAPY, and with the addition of anti-depressant medication, I began to feel a great, heavy cloak slowly lifting off of me, a garment I didn't even know I was wearing, the wet, woolen scent of it slowly evaporating from the pores of my skin. I began to see my life in nuances of color instead of a flat, monotonous gray. I began to feel a variety of emotions I had not been able to feel. I wanted to be a person who could live and feel in color. I wanted it for myself and for my family, especially my children. I didn't want them to continue to grow up with a mother who was emotionally distant because she didn't know how to allow herself to feel what she felt.

My therapist told me therapy can be likened to taking your car to the mechanic. Some people come in for a tune-up, a small adjustment in one area of their life, perhaps a few tweaks so the bumpy ride might smooth out a bit. But what I needed, he advised, was a major overhaul; the whole engine needed to be rebuilt.

So we engaged in the same kind of work my husband and I were doing with our old home. We began the dismantling process of myself, sifting through all that was there, deciding what needed to be discarded, and choosing what to salvage and integrate into my new self.

From my very early years, I had been told who to be (seen but not heard) and who not to be (someone with an opinion). I had been told how to feel (happy, content) and how not to feel (sad, angry). I became accustomed to believing that others' perspectives and opinions about myself mattered more than my own. I believed if I became who I was told to be, that would be my ticket to being loved—or at the very least, not abandoned.

It was a lesson in becoming small.

I was like the little boy, Claude, in the novel *This Is How It*

Always Is, who kept drawing pictures where he appeared smaller and smaller until, finally, he was no longer there at all.[2]

In therapy I had to sift through a lot of detritus and dung that had clung to me for many years: old ways of thinking, coping mechanisms that no longer served me. What if I sifted through everything and found nothing worth keeping? Would this process be worth it?

In the Christian Scriptures there is a story where Jesus asked a sick man, "Do you want to be made well?" The man didn't respond with a yes or a no. Instead, he told Jesus all the things getting in his way of being made well.[3] I resonate with this story because so many things got in my way of being made emotionally well, things I thought protected me. Things that *had* protected me at one time, like not taking up too much room, trying not to be noticed, staying small, quiet. Eventually, though, these things got in the way. Once the depression started to lift, I could see this more clearly.

So I undertook the hard work—and underneath all the rubble, I found parts of myself I wanted to salvage. I discovered my inquisitive self, the child in elementary school who kept asking the *why* questions about the things we learned, wanting to find the answers underneath the answers. I discovered my creative self who, when I was twelve or thirteen, began to write poems and even had one published in a teen magazine. I discovered the gift of my intellectual self, the one who set the curve on my college biochemistry final, much to the dismay of my classmates.

I remembered that at some point during my childhood, I had wanted to become an architect. I spent hours drawing floor plans, imagining the homes that could be built and the families who would inhabit them. Somewhere along the way, that memory was lost. But as it resurfaced during therapy, I marveled at what had transpired when we initially made the decision to rebuild our home.

We had gone through a frustrating process of hiring several different architects to draw up our house plans, with none of them fully capturing our vision. Finally, at wit's end, I proclaimed I would draw the plans myself. Since I knew exactly what we wanted, I thought I could easily create the blueprints of our family home. And I did. I didn't know at the time that I was also responding to my authentic self's yearning to be unburied.

Underneath all the rubble, underneath all the detritus and dung, I discovered my authentic self—my imaginative, creative, inquisitive, intelligent self.

But in sorting through it all, I also bumped into uninvited guests, guests I had unknowingly harbored for quite some time. These guests were memories my mind had pushed far, far away but my body remembered. My body held those memories until I was emotionally well enough, and safe enough, to recall them.

Memories of incest from throughout my childhood.

WHEN THE MEMORIES SURFACED, I was afraid to confront my dad about his transgressions, but I knew I had to do something. Say something. Although my parents lived several states away, almost eight hundred miles, we kept in touch frequently by phone and saw each other several times a year at least. I couldn't act like nothing had happened.

I had recently told them I was seeing a counselor, "working through some things," but I felt more and more anxious when I talked with them. I started avoiding their calls. I wanted to figure out how to broach this with them. Meanwhile, they became more solicitous toward me. On the day of my thirty-seventh birthday, they called several times, but I didn't pick up. The next morning, when the phone rang and the caller ID showed it was them *again*, I was so frustrated that I answered the call.

It was my mom wishing me a happy belated birthday, asking why I didn't respond to her calls the previous day. Without meaning to, with no prior strategy on my part, I blurted out that I had been remembering some hard memories from my childhood, memories that involved Dad.

I heard a sharp intake of breath. Then in a clipped voice, she said, "I can't *believe* you are going to bring this up, after all these years. Do you have *any idea* how this will affect your father?"

I felt her words like a physical blow. A punch to my gut. The wind knocked out of me. I took the receiver away from my ear and stared at it.

She knew.

When I got my breath again, I brought the receiver back to my ear and uttered, "What about me, Mom? What about me?"

Then I hung up the phone.

Not too long after that, I received a letter in the mail from my dad. He wasn't angry, he wrote, but he was disappointed I could believe these things about him. He wasn't angry, he reiterated, because he could understand how I was confused, being in therapy and not in my right mind. He suggested I consider finding a new counselor, one who could better help me with my mental problems.

He was trying to make me think I didn't know what I was talking about. He was trying to make me small. Again.

Had he ever really stopped?

He wanted the real me, who knew the real truth, to disappear.

But I was doing the very hard emotional work of claiming

who I am: dismantling the old ways, discovering my authentic self, creating a new path. I didn't want to be small anymore. I didn't want to disappear.

I chose not to respond to the letter. I chose not to call either of my parents. It was the only way I could hold on to my sense of self.

We never spoke again.

I was in therapy a good, long while after that. These were not wounds I could cover with a bandage or even stitch together with sutures. These wounds cut so deep, the only way for them to heal was to let them breathe, to expose them to the warm light and the fresh air of compassion and care.

And it saved me.

The incredibly grueling, grief-filled work of becoming emotionally well saved me.

I wrote a poem during that time about my desire to claim and live into the freedom of this new reality, the wholeness of my authentic self. It was the first poem I had written since I was a teenager.

Freedom of the Dolphin

Teach me the freedom of the dolphin.
Release my spirit to dance like her in the waters of light.
With hardly a whisper she sails through the sea,
her presence revealed only by the rippling water.
Soaring upward, she is drawn to the source
of the warmth she feels,
warmth which penetrates even the depths of the sea.
Beautifully arched, she hangs suspended
an eternal second
before gliding back into the sea,
full of joy, full of grace.

The mystery of the freedom of the dolphin
is in the very nature of her moving, her being.
Her spirit does the bidding;
her heart and mind and body
follow as one.

Teach me the freedom of the dolphin.
Impress upon my heart and mind and body
to follow my spirit.
Arouse in my spirit the desire
to hear your whisper,
the whisper of your Spirit,
so I may know the freedom of the dolphin,
until all that I am,
all that is freedom—
courage and peace and passion and
joy and love and grace—
all that I am created to be
is released in my spirit
to dance in the waters of light.

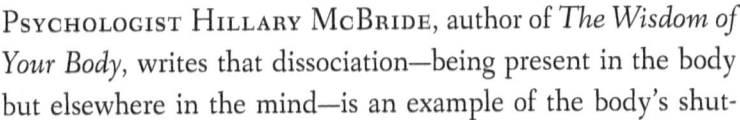

PSYCHOLOGIST HILLARY McBRIDE, author of *The Wisdom of Your Body*, writes that dissociation—being present in the body but elsewhere in the mind—is an example of the body's shutdown response:

> When it comes to the shutdown response, there is no [conscious] choice at all. It is completely automatic. Shutting down does not mean that you are weak or that the trauma is not real—it means your nervous system is the one calling the shots. . . . A brain-body system that learned it couldn't survive

by staying engaged, running away, or fighting back decides its best strategy is to shut down and disengage.[4]

This explained why I had no previous recollection of the trauma. My body saved me by taking the brunt of it, allowing my mind to dissociate entirely.

As the memories surfaced and I worked through them in the safety of my counselor's reassuring and trusted presence, I began to heal not only emotionally and mentally but also physically. The nerve pain in my face improved, gradually dissipating altogether. No other medical issues cropped up in its place.

I became physically well.

At some point I realized Peter had been right. All my physical ailments were due to the trauma held within. My body had protected me for decades by holding the memories until she felt I was ready to accept them. Then she spoke up, telling me it was time to let the unbearable truth of my childhood come to light. My body had carried the weight of it all this time, unbeknownst to my conscious self.

But I had a really good reason not to listen to her, a really good reason to adamantly *resist* listening to her. I was meant to be keeping a secret, a secret I was led to believe would have devastating consequences if ever revealed.

As children, when the people in our lives who are supposed to love us the most are the ones who cause us traumatic harm, it leaves us feeling like we are not lovable. That we are not *worthy* of being loved. Otherwise, we reason, they would not harm us this way. This is the logic of children. Our perpetrators capitalize on this, warning us that if we ever tell, no one will ever love us. As John Meyers, an expert on child maltreatment, explains:

For sexually abused children, physical injury is seldom the problem. The body of the physically or sexually abused child usually survives intact. But the child's essential sense of self-worth, his or her inner soul, may be damaged for life by the psychological abuse that lies at the heart of physical and sexual abuse.[5]

I wasn't able to listen to my body's attempts to get me to look at nonphysical causes of my medical issues because underneath it all, I carried a deep sense of shame that I was inherently unlovable. Shame—the belief that there is something fundamentally wrong with you—is a powerful motivator to keep silent.

But my body knew the truth of what happened to me. To *us*. She carried that reality.

She carried another reality too. It is the sacred truth woven into our bones from the beginning of time. As human beings, created from the dust of the earth and endowed with the breath of the divine, each of us has inherent worth. Unconditional and nonnegotiable. Our worth doesn't change just because someone treats us like we're unworthy.

All this time, I had believed a lie. As a result, I had spent my life striving to earn my worth, not realizing I was pushing back against the lie, trying to overcome it by showing that I *am* worth something. I earnestly endeavored to be the perfect daughter, the perfect student, the perfect athlete, that I might show my father I was worthy of being loved. Growing into adulthood, still bound by the lie, I was determined to be the perfect wife and the perfect mother. I would show everyone I was worth something.

This is a burden that only gets heavier with time, when we try to earn our worth rather than receive the birthright that is ours to claim. By the time my third child arrived, it became too much to bear.

I always told myself it was my inability to be the perfect mother to my three little children that led to the memories finding their way to the surface. But recently, when I shared this story in my writers' group, my friend Kathryn—who knows my whole story—said, "Maybe it wasn't because of your *weakness* as a mother of three, but because of your *strength* as a mother of three. Maybe your body noticed how you lovingly advocated for your young children, and she knew she could entrust you to advocate for your own young self."

This had never occurred to me before.

The more I reflected on Kathryn's observation, the more I resonated with the wisdom of her words. My body had witnessed how I learned to advocate for my children. She knew I was finally strong enough to face the memories and all that came with them. So she spoke up on my behalf. And she kept speaking until I could claim the courage to seek the truth.

She saved me. My body saved me.

Chapter 5

My Three Dreams

Thread of Light: Come home to yourself

I had a dream I was in a hospital room, standing by the bed of someone I didn't know. We were talking about spiritual matters. When I awoke, I felt this surprisingly strong sense that this was what I was meant to do. This was my vocational calling.

Over the previous six months, as I worked through my depression and could see my life more clearly, I had been wondering about my vocation and beginning to discern what was next for me. April would start first grade in the fall, bringing my season as a stay-at-home mom to an end. I had kept up my credentials as a registered and licensed dietitian (my vocation prior to the arrival of children), always with the plan that I would return to that work. The field had evolved over the years I was away, and there seemed to be more opportunities available. I had been a renal dietitian before, taking care of patients with chronic kidney failure, and although the work was intellectually stimulating and relationally engaging, I thought that moving forward I'd like to work with healthy populations, maybe in pediatric nutrition or sports nutrition.

But a few months before I had the hospital dream, while talking to Jay about my discernment, I asked his opinion on where he could see me working. I remember we were in the car, driving along the coast, headed north on A1A.

He glanced over at me, then turned his eyes back to the road.

I knew him well enough to know he was gathering his thoughts, which could sometimes take a few minutes. I looked out my window at the rough ocean surf.

Finally, he said, "You know what? I don't know if working in nutrition is what's next for you. For some reason, I think God might be calling you to become a pastor."

What?

I laughed. I actually laughed. Like Sarah in the Book of Genesis when she heard she would bear a child in her old age.[1] It seemed absurd. Yet I trusted my husband when he spoke about God. He was a man of faith. We had grown together in our faith journeys since our high school days. Our love for God was foundational to our love for one another. Our commitment to God was foundational to our commitment to one another.

Was there some truth to what he said? Was God calling me to become a pastor?

I started having dreams about it. In my first dream, I stood in front of a crowd of young people in a big room, preaching to them.

Oh dear, I thought, once I woke. *Is God calling me to be a youth pastor?*

The idea of working with teenagers terrified me; Wilson

was not yet ten at the time. When I told Jay about my dream, he proclaimed, "That wasn't a dream; it was a nightmare!"

But compared to my next dream, the youth pastor dream seemed tame. In the next dream, I was preaching in my home church, a sanctuary that easily holds five hundred people. It was packed that day, and as I stood in the pulpit and looked out over the vast congregation, every single face staring back at me was my father's. I woke up in a sweat, heart pounding.

Now *that* was a nightmare.

Maybe Jay was wrong about me being a pastor, because there was no way I would willingly submit myself to that kind of scrutiny and silent mockery by older, authoritative men. It felt like they were vultures ready to consume me.

But then I had the third dream, the dream where I stood by the hospital bed of a patient, having a spiritual conversation with them. It all felt so natural, like I'd been doing it all my life. It was a peace-filled dream that left me feeling calm and settled. I interpreted the dream to mean that God was calling me to become a hospital chaplain.

This time when I told Jay about my dream, he nodded like we'd finally solved a puzzle. "Yes," he said, clapping his hands together. "That's it. That's what you're meant to do." When I ventured to share my sense of calling with a few trusted friends, they too affirmed and supported my revelation.

I began to look into the credentials I would need to become a hospital chaplain and learned I would need to be ordained, which in my denomination required a Master of Divinity degree, a three-year graduate program. If God was calling me to become a chaplain, did that mean God was also calling me to become ordained? I really didn't know. So I went to talk to my pastor, who shared that the discernment process for ordination in the United Methodist Church was a long and winding road set up to help people like me figure out our sense of call. He told me I could take the first step and then, as I felt led, the next step and then the next and so on. Eventually, he assured me, I would gain clarity on which way I was being called.

At the time, seminary felt like the next right step, and I was confident that even if the path didn't lead to ordination, I could still use my degree. I began applying to seminaries. But then the repressed memories started coming up, and I was no longer sure seminary was a good idea. I thought seminarians should have it all together, and I felt like I was back to falling apart. Not only did I feel emotionally fragile, but I was beginning to feel spiritually drained. All that I had thought to be true about my family of origin was crumbling, and this led me to question all I had thought to be true about my faith. When certainty about one area of life is on shaky ground, it leads to speculating if *any* area of life is sturdy. I wondered if I should put seminary off, at least for now, so I could focus on therapy.

My counselor encouraged me to go ahead with my educational plans. In addition to being a mental health counselor, he was an ordained minister, so he knew seminarians didn't have it all together. He also knew seminaries had the potential to be sanctuaries of fertile soil for one to dig through faith-related questions. He thought seminary would contribute to my healing.

And it did.

Seminary called forth those parts of myself that I was salvaging through my therapy process: the intellectual, creative, imaginative, and inquisitive aspects of my authentic self. I knew I was smart, but I also knew I had worked hard academically. It wasn't until I went to seminary that I recognized my intellect was a gift, one I could enjoy as well as use in service to others. Also, I was pleased to discover seminary was not just about learning facts, like my studies in nutrition and dietetics had been. My professors wanted to know what I thought about

God and humanity, and why. They wanted to know how I would integrate my theology into my life and help others do the same.

The whole academic enterprise engaged my inquisitive, imaginative, and creative capabilities. It was like seminary affirmed and celebrated all those parts of myself I had recently reclaimed. By the time I was ready to graduate from seminary (which took me five years instead of three because I was also a full-time mom), I knew I was also ready to graduate from my therapy work. The two had dovetailed beautifully.

I also gained the clarity that ordained ministry was the path for me.

My seminary journey deepened and broadened my understanding of my vocational calling, and several years after graduation, when an opportunity opened up for a chaplain at a local university, I thought, *Why not?* It sounded like it would be more fun than hospital chaplaincy, as I'd be working with people who were healthy rather than those who were sick. I applied and, after several interviews, was offered the position.

Interestingly, I ended up spending a fair amount of time at the hospital in my new role, visiting students who had been in accidents or were ill. And for the first two years, I led a weekly chapel service for the students, where I preached. I was responsible for the prayers at convocation and graduation, too, sitting up on the speakers' platform with mostly older men in authoritative positions at the university. These things weren't all I did, but it was enough to bring to mind my three dreams. Perhaps God had spoken to me through *all* the dreams, but I couldn't envision myself as a pastor until I stood by the hospital bed. I've often wondered if that was because I felt at home in hospitals, having spent so much time in them in my work as a dietitian, that the Spirit of God found a way to graciously ease me into recognizing my future as an ordained minister.

In my work as a university chaplain, I encountered students from all over the world, from so many different cultures, religions, and beliefs. Muslim students from Saudi Arabia. Hindu and Sikh students from India. Jewish students from Israel. Buddhist students from South Korea, Thailand, and Japan. Of course, it wasn't so neat and tidy like that. There were Catholic students from India and Christian students from South Korea and students from the United States who claimed all these religious identities as well. There were students who were atheist, agnostic, and humanist. And those who identified as spiritual but not religious or who identified as spiritual with no qualifier or disclaimer attached.

When I began my tenure as a chaplain, my philosophy was to honor and value each person I encountered, regardless of his or her faith identity or belief system. I believed the essence of being a chaplain was to reflect God's unconditional acceptance of humanity by accepting others in this way. My commitment to this philosophy deepened through my day-to-day work as a chaplain, and my interactions with students from diverse religious beliefs cultivated in me a worldview of a more inclusive God and a more expansive spirituality.

This spurred in me a desire to foster a healthy interfaith community on campus, which included advocating for those who claimed no religious identity. I began to explore what spirituality looked like when it wasn't a part of a faith tradition and how I might nurture the spiritual life of those who were not religious.

I went on a search to find a definition for the word *spiritual* that was independent of religious connotations. What I found was there was no universally agreed upon way to define it. So I pored over all the information I had gathered and crafted my own definition: *spiritual* refers to that part of ourselves—our spirit—that seeks connection, meaning, and purpose.

The process of sorting this out helped me appreciate that every one of us has that piece within us; *everyone* has a spirit. For some, nurturing their spirit might include connecting with God through a religious community. For others, it might involve connecting with God without religious practices. And for still others, it may not be about religion or God at all.

When I look back over my time as a university chaplain, I can now recognize a shift that occurred in my own relationship between religion and spirituality. For much of my faith journey, I had lived my spirituality within the context of my religion. My spiritual practices, for the most part, were connected with my church: Sunday worship, midweek Bible study, corporate prayer, fellowship, service. But through my work on campus, where the waters of religion and spirituality commingled, my understanding of spiritual practice became much broader. Watching how students from different religious traditions—or no tradition at all—found meaning, purpose, and connection in their lives inspired me to pay more attention to the spiritual nature of *my* everyday life.

I couldn't see it then, but a shift also occurred in Jay. A different shift. A shift away from the values that had been formational to our relationship and our marriage. While I lived more deeply into my ministerial calling, he drifted away from spiritual things. More than a decade earlier, when he first suggested a pastoral vocation for me, we were together on that two-lane coastal road, aligned and headed in the same direction. But somewhere along the way, he turned toward a different road, one that carried him further and further away.

DURING MY SIXTH year at the university, I began to feel a restlessness in my spirit, which surprised me. I thought I loved my work. But on reflection, I acknowledged to myself that I felt drained by the pastoral care—visiting injured students in the hospital, leading memorial services for deceased students, offering consolation to students whose parents were diagnosed with terminal illnesses. The bad things that could happen in the course of an ordinary day seemed unrelenting. I thought I practiced good self-care, but compassion fatigue has a way of creeping up on you, seeping into you, undetected.

And there were things going on in my marriage that I wasn't letting myself pay attention to. Had these things seeped into my work? How much energy had it required to keep them at bay?

Eventually, I met with my clergy supervisor, who gently suggested perhaps it was time to leave my role as university chaplain. I knew deep in my spirit that if I left the university, I would also leave chaplaincy behind forever. I had identified myself as a college chaplain for more than six years, and I loved that identity. But if I were being honest with myself, I no longer loved the work. Which was hard for me to fathom because I had been so gifted for it. And called to it.

If I was no longer a chaplain, what was my calling now?

In the year that followed my resignation from the university, I enrolled in a series of four retreats for clergy in my geographical area. The purpose of these retreats was to help us learn how to connect our role to our soul as clergy leaders. The retreats were based on the work of Parker Palmer, who writes:

> Our deepest calling is to grow into our own authentic self-hood, whether or not it conforms to some image of who we *ought* to be. As we do so, we will not only find the joy that every human being seeks—we will also find our path of authentic service in the world.[2]

I discovered my calling was meant to be more about who I am (my soul) rather than what I do (my role). This new understanding helped me realize that chaplaincy had been a *container* for my vocational calling, not the calling itself. How could I begin to identify myself not by my role but by my soul?

The time of intense reflection at the retreats brought me back to those aspects of my authentic self—my introspective, inquisitive, creative self—that I had reclaimed through therapy and celebrated through seminary but had somehow let slip into the background of my life in the intervening years. Life had been busy since graduating from seminary, with working at the university while also mothering my three children through high school and college and trying to keep up with the expanding social demands of my husband's schedule. I had not had much space to claim as my own, and this is what my soul craved.

Through these retreats, I also came to acknowledge my shyness. I had always tried to hide it because my family of origin taunted me about it, as if being shy were a personality defect. Shyness is not a quality people look for in a clergyperson; I had attempted to cover it up so I could present what others expected of my role. But I began to understand that *shy* does not necessarily mean timid or afraid, that it can be more about a quiet and reserved nature. One who thinks before she speaks. One who doesn't have to speak to be present. One who has a contemplative posture toward life and the world. I began to understand my shyness could be a gift rather than a liability.

In claiming my shyness, I was making an assertion to resist conforming to the expectations of others. I liked the idea of a part of me remaining untamed and how my untamed shyness could keep me in tune with my true feelings. As I embraced my shyness, I felt like I embraced my authentic self.

I thought back to my work at the university, about the students who were atheist, agnostic, and humanist. I thought about the ones who had left religion or were never a part of it to begin with. Many of them still sought to live authentic lives full of connection, meaning, and purpose, but often they were dismissed by those who were religious as having no spiritual integrity. It made me wonder if my desire to be my authentic shy self was why I had been acutely aware of those who desired to be their authentic spiritual selves. My heart had always gone out to them. I saw how they longed to nurture their spirit without all the trappings of religion. I wanted to affirm and celebrate that in them. I wanted to advocate for them.

I began to see that perhaps this was my calling, and had been my calling all along: to notice and affirm, to encourage and nurture the spiritual life of those who were not religious.

But what would be the next container for my vocational calling?

I was as surprised as I had been with my hospital dream to discern that creative spiritual writing wanted to be the next expression, the next container, for my vocational calling. This clarity came about as I reflected on when I had been my most authentic self during my tenure as a university chaplain.

My mind traveled back to the many liturgies and meditations I wrote for the memorial services I officiated for deceased students, staff, and faculty. I recognized my innate gift to create beauty out of words, beauty that somehow conveyed comfort and peace and hope to those who mourned. I was reminded of all the prayers I had written for university events and how my words helped others to connect with the sacred in the midst of secular observances. I thought of the biweekly column I wrote for the school newspaper about seeking the spiritual in the everyday. I thought of my chapel assistant, who told me, "I always knew you were passionate about writing."

It was a hard transition trying to figure out what a "writing ministry" could look like, but I felt a sense of peace in having the spaciousness for quiet contemplation and reflective writing. It felt like the different parts of my authentic self all had the space to stretch out and grow while helping others do the same. I resonated with the words of Natalie Goldberg, author of *The True Secret of Writing: Connecting Life With Language*: "To find your writer's voice is to find your spine; it is to connect your breath of inspiration with the world's breath."[3]

Six months into my writing ministry—and *sixteen years* after my three dreams—I found myself in marriage counseling at the behest of my husband. He wasn't happy, he said, and I was the reason why. His chief complaint? He wanted me to be more social.

This had been a thread of tension throughout our marriage. As an extrovert, he drew energy from being around others. As an introvert, I drew energy by being alone. Socially, I preferred quiet, intimate gatherings, like dinner with another couple or perhaps a small dinner party. I wanted to connect with people on a deeper level than just small talk. Jay's idea of a social gathering was to regularly throw pig roasts in our backyard and invite everyone we knew, and sometimes even people I didn't know. Often there would be more than a hundred guests at these events.

We had gone to counseling earlier in our marriage to work through our conflict around this, and we learned ways to compromise. We vowed to honor each other's nature and desires, and we worked on our social calendar to reflect this.

But now it all felt different. How he defined *social* was different than before. It no longer was about get-togethers in the backyard; it was about going with his new group of friends to loud concerts, busy bars, and crowded parties. It might have been tolerable for my introverted soul if he hadn't mostly ignored me, but he seemed to resent my presence. He was like an adolescent who didn't want anyone to know his parents made him bring his younger sister along. He'd run off with his friends, and I was left standing there, wondering, *Why am I here?*

My chief complaint? I wanted him to be the person he used to be. I was angry that the kind, gentle, spiritual man I had known and loved more than half my life had somehow morphed into someone I no longer recognized.

When did this happen? And where was my husband?

Jay and I used to joke with each other that I was the scuba diver and he was the snorkeler in our relationship because I always wanted us to go deep in our conversations and he preferred to skim the surface. As I thought about this, I realized that in recent years, it seemed like he had become more and more reticent to go deep when prompted, and I had grown more and more weary with the effort.

When had I resigned myself to a snorkeling-level marriage?

Marriage counseling brought to light the fundamental differences in how we wanted to live our lives. It became clear to me that we no longer shared the same values. Despite this, despite the erosion of our relationship, despite my diminished sense of self, I wanted to stay married. Couldn't we just pretend all was well, even if it wasn't? If we divorced, then everyone would know we couldn't make our marriage work. Everyone would know I couldn't be the wife he wanted me to be.

Our marriage counselor told us research indicated a majority of couples were unhappy in their marriages but stayed married anyway. After she said that, I thought, *And one day one of them will die, and the widowed one will receive sympathy for losing the love of their life, never having to reveal the state of their marriage.*

Why couldn't we stay married so one day I could be a widow who received sympathy, rather than a divorcée who received judgment?

Underneath all of this was a deep-seated, unspoken fear. I wanted to stay married because I believed our thirty-three-year marriage provided the framework that held me together. My marital role of wife was an all-encompassing identity that had enveloped my life—my being, my very essence—since I was twenty years old. I was afraid there would be nothing left of me if I had to give that up.

But the spool of my marriage unwound anyway, and I watched the fabric of my life flutter away, right before my very eyes.

WHEN I FINALLY CAME UP FOR air on the other side of the long divorce process, I became conscious that my vocational calling was patiently waiting for me, graciously waiting to remind me of who I am and how I'm called to bear light in the world.

Oh, how I had forsaken myself.

Although I still grieved so much—a whole life lost to me, an entire way of living gone down with the ship—I slowly breathed in new air. Fresh air. This gave me the capacity to lean more fully into my introverted, introspective nature, affirming and nurturing my creative, imaginative, inquisitive self.

While I thought I had lost everything, what I eventually discovered as I traversed that long and winding road was that my vocational calling had called me home to myself. She had been calling me home all along the way.

Chapter 6

A Bear, a Hurricane, and an Obituary

Thread of Light: Notice new ways to be a family

S ix weeks after saving the drowning armadillo, I packed Bear and Skye into my little red station wagon and moved seven miles north of town. Initially, I had wanted to keep our family home, the home that had raised my children, the home they had returned to during college breaks and even after. They grew up believing they would always have their family home to come back to, no matter how old they grew or how far they roamed.

And, in my mind's eye, I had imagined it would be the home my future grandchildren would come to know and adore, sleeping in the same beds their parents slept in as children, playing in the same rooms, exploring the same backyard. Every time I thought about selling it, I felt like a piece of my heart withered up and died.

But there were too many happy family memories in that

house, and it made me so incredibly sad to be reminded of them. I saw ghosts of our life together everywhere: lounging on the front porch, laughing around the dinner table, enjoying an evening by the chiminea. But they were only ghosts now; with the impending divorce, it felt like all the life had been sucked out of my beloved home.

The kids were all in their twenties and living on their own. April was all the way down in Argentina, living and working there. Although Wilson and Meredith lived nearby, they didn't come around as much since the separation. I knew it was hard for them, too, to be in our family home now. And I knew they also wanted to spend time with their dad up at his beach house, forty-five minutes north of town. It used to be *our* beach house, but it became his when we separated. Now I was all alone, except for the ghosts. It was too much for my battered spirit, and I finally decided the best way for me to heal would be to move house.

But where? I had lived in this town almost thirty years, in this house for twenty-four of them. Where would I go? Should I stay downtown, in the historic district, in my neighborhood close to the river, where I had watched the sun rise every morning for decades? That would be most familiar. But maybe too familiar. Too sad.

I knew I didn't want to go any further west; I wanted to stay near the water. And that's when I thought maybe the beachside —the long, skinny barrier island between the river and the ocean—would be a welcome change in the midst of all my upheaval. I began driving up and down A1A, checking out neighborhoods and going to open houses. The further north I drove, the more settled I felt. The businesses thinned out, the traffic lessened, the island narrowed, and the view of the ocean opened up right beside the road.

I felt my stale breath, too long held in, shudder out. And on the inhale, I breathed in the salty surf air and felt parts of me begin to soften ever so slightly—my hunched shoulders, my clenched jaw, my knotted gut.

Back when Jay and I were looking to buy our first home, we received advice from a friend who was older and wiser. She said, "Always fall in love with a neighborhood first. Then find a home you can love within that neighborhood." So that's what I did. When I had gone as far north as I could go without wandering into the next county, I discovered a neighborhood nestled between the river and the ocean where the island was less than half a mile wide. It was relatively new, and I learned from my realtor most of the residents were from somewhere else . . . New York, New Jersey, New England. I liked that. They wouldn't know the history that was shared by so many of us in town, those of us who met as young couples, raised our children together, became empty nesters together. They wouldn't know the saga of my fractured family. And I wouldn't have to be reminded of families going about their family lives; I could tell this little neighborhood was primarily older retirees, who probably had left their grown children living up north where they raised them.

Two homes for sale in the neighborhood were within my budget. I made an appointment with my realtor to look at them and asked Meredith to come with me. The first house we toured felt like a good fit for me living on my own. Everything was cozy small, from the kitchen to the living area to the postage-stamp-sized backyard. With the low ceilings and lack of natural light, I felt like I would be as "snug as a bug in a rug" living there.

"But *Mom*," Meredith cried, "there's no room for any of us! Where will we all sit when we come over?"

I hadn't considered this. I wasn't looking for a family home, because I felt like I no longer had a family. I wanted something big enough for one, something that would wrap me up, cocoon-like. Not something with enough space to remind me who wasn't there.

The second home we toured was only slightly larger, in terms of square footage, but it felt more spacious because of the vaulted ceilings and windows everywhere. Light streamed in. If the first home felt like it would hold me in a warm hug, this one felt like it would give me room to breathe, to let my lungs expand, to take up space.

I wouldn't have to try to be small anymore, to fit myself into someone else's life.

Meredith was captivated as soon as she walked through the front door. "*This* is your home, Mom. This is *so* you."

That is how I came to buy the home on Heron Dunes Drive, seven miles north of town. I would learn these seven miles weren't a "hop on the interstate for a quick trip up the road" kind of seven miles. Rather, they were a "cross over the bridge and creep your way up A1A, the two-lane coastal road with double yellow lines running down the center of it *the entire seven miles*, where you might get stuck behind someone going thirty miles an hour" kind of seven miles north of town. The kids joked I might as well have moved to Georgia, it felt so far away.

But that's because our family home was in the center of town and it never took us any longer than five minutes to get anywhere. But alas, our family home was in *the center of town*, where everyone knew my business. I loved the idea of removing myself from all the talk swirling around me.

Once I decided to make an offer on the Heron Dunes house, I went to sign the contract at my realtor's office—and felt a bolt of shock at the two signature lines for buyers at the bottom of the document. Of course, there would be space for two signatures, for a couple, two partners, purchasing a home together. The reality of my circumstances seared my heart. I was on my own now.

$$\sim$$

Jay and I had divided all our belongings, sorting them into categories of what I wanted, what he wanted, what each of the kids wanted, and what no one wanted. Furniture, linens, dishes, knickknacks, books, wine. In the category of what no one wanted: our wedding china, my wedding dress, the Lladró porcelain figurine of a bride and groom that had been a wedding gift. Who wanted reminders of a marriage that failed? Who wanted reminders of a time we started a life together, so full of promise and hope?

April flew back from Argentina for a few weeks to say goodbye to her childhood home and help me with the move. I'll never forget that first morning in my new kitchen, how she took charge as I stood in the midst of all the boxes, turning around, not knowing where to begin. It felt like a metaphor for the chaos of my life. How did I get here? And how do I begin to make some sense of all of it? April walked in, clapped her hands together, and said, "Okay! Let's get started. This is what we'll do first." And she set about giving me some much-needed direction for my new life by helping me organize my new kitchen.

Three days later, in the evening, April was back in one of the guest rooms while I sat on the couch with my feet propped on the coffee table, emotionally and physically exhausted after the long days of unpacking and sorting. There were boxes and boxes of my books stacked four and five high, creating unintended makeshift walls in the living and dining areas. I hadn't unpacked any of them because there was nowhere to put them. I had grossly overestimated the space in this house and grossly underestimated how many books I owned. I would need to cull through them again.

I had just begun to relax when I heard a noise, a clattering of sorts, on the other side of the wall of boxes.

"April, is that you?" I called, too tired to get up.

No answer.

It must be the dogs, I thought, *wrestling with one another*. This house was so much smaller than what they were accustomed to, the backyard too, and they'd been restless since I moved in. The old family home had been the only home they knew.

"Bear! Skye! That's enough. Time to chill out."

But the racket increased just as Skye came into view, looking at me intently. Surprised, I got up to see what was going on.

I discovered Bear laid out on the floor, body stiff but legs flailing, paddling furiously like a horse in a wild river current, head knocking about.

"April! Come quick! Something's wrong with Bear!"

I'd never seen anyone—much less a dog—have a seizure, so I wasn't sure that's what this was, but it certainly didn't look like the twitches that occurred when he had a dream.

"Oh my gosh, Mom!" April exclaimed as she came into the room. "We need to do something. We need to help him."

"I don't know what to do. I don't . . . I don't . . . I don't know . . . wh-what to do." I just stood there, staring and stammering over my words.

"Is it a seizure? Do you think it's a seizure?" she asked.

"I don't know, I don't know," I said, my words running together. "We need to do *something*, but I don't know what to do."

I started talking to Bear in a soothing voice—"It's okay, buddy, it's okay"—but he paid no attention. He was somewhere else. Skye looked on cautiously. April took charge. Thank God.

She said, "I don't think you're supposed to do anything when someone's having a seizure. You just have to wait for it to stop. When he stops . . . *if* . . . *when* . . . he stops, we need to get him to an emergency clinic."

"But where?" I said. "Look at me, living in the middle of godforsaken nowhere! Why'd I move *here* of all places? I have no idea where the closest emergency clinic is. I should know this. I should have figured this out before I moved here." I was frantic.

"Just hold on, Mom," April said, holding her phone. "I'm googling it. I got it. There's one up in Flagler—ten, fifteen minutes away. Let's go there."

Thank God for April, whose phone is an appendage, whose first instinct is to google.

"Okay, but you drive," I said. "You have to drive. I can't drive. I'll sit in the back with Bear. Oh my goodness, Bear. How are we even going to get him in the car?"

I hadn't taken my eyes off him. He was still thrashing. How long had it been? Two minutes? Three? Five?

Neither of us said anything. We waited forever.

Eventually, I asked, "Does he look like he's slowing down to you? I think he might be slowing down."

April confirmed. "Yeah, I think so too. I'm gonna call the clinic, let them know we're heading there."

"Okay. Okay. Okay." I kept repeating myself, watching and waiting, willing Bear to come to.

The seizure finally seemed to loosen its grip on him, and he lay slumped on the floor.

"Hey, Bear Dog. Hey, buddy," I whispered as I squatted next to him and stroked his back. He looked around like he didn't know where he was, didn't know who I was. I could hear

April on the phone. Skye had lost interest and wandered off amid the boxes. "It's gonna be all right, buddy. You're gonna be okay."

We called the other kids on the way to the animal hospital. Wilson, Meredith, and Meredith's husband, Anthony, worked for the same company and were together that night at a work-related event. They said they'd leave immediately and meet us there. When the vet walked into the crowded exam room, he tried to hide his surprise at seeing all of us there: April and me in ratty T-shirts and shorts, Wilson and Anthony in suits and ties, Meredith in a cocktail dress and heels. It was hard for him to locate his groggy patient tucked in among us all. But one thing was abundantly clear to him: Bear was our beloved family dog.

He asked us questions about what happened and about Bear's medical history. Bear had a rich and colorful history of what our family vet had labeled "dietary indiscretions." He always seemed to get himself into some kind of digestive trouble because of things he ate when no one was looking, such as the charcoal briquettes out by the grill, the chocolates in the Christmas stockings, the kids' sweaty socks they peeled off and abandoned when they returned from their athletic endeavors. Bear was a stealthy and swift counter surfer who could snatch a piece of pizza or a sandwich when its owner left it unattended momentarily while reaching into the fridge for a drink. Bear was known for this kind of thing, but bona fide medical issues? No, we told the vet. Bear had no chronic medical issues.

Nodding, he examined Bear, then took him to the back to do some blood work. When the vet returned, he said the blood work looked good and that based on Bear's advanced age (he was eleven years old) and this being his first seizure, the most likely diagnosis was a brain tumor.

We looked at one another, shaking our heads, talking over one another in our disbelief.

"A *brain tumor?*"

"No, no, that can't be."

"Not Bear."

"He hasn't had any other symptoms to suggest this."

"It has to be a one-off. A fluke."

The vet looked dubiously at us, his eyes scanning back and forth between us. I think he was trying to identify who among us might not be in denial. Apparently, not one of us was prepared to accept this news.

Finally, he spoke slowly and clearly (as if that would bring us around). "Usually when a dog this age who has no history of seizures has a seizure of this magnitude . . . in most cases, it is because he has a brain tumor. Which means . . . that most likely . . . he will continue to have seizures." He let that hang in the air, but we couldn't capture it.

He continued, "We can send him to Gainesville, to the vet school, where they can do an MRI of his brain, and then we will know for sure."

"*Gainesville?*"

"An MRI?"

It was too much. Gainesville, two hours away, was where I went for my brain surgery. It was where people went who had the most serious of medical concerns, because the University of Florida hospital system located there had the capability to address those concerns. It was the same for animals. The UF vet school was top-notch in its capacity to treat the most severe of canine injuries, illnesses, and diseases. It was too much to consider Bear needed that kind of medical attention.

The kids looked at me for direction. I looked at Wilson for a sense of what to do. After all, Wilson was Bear's favorite. He was Bear's boy. Those two had a special connection. But

Wilson looked at me, deferring to me. The vet also looked at me as the elder in our group. Now, all of a sudden, I was in charge. The mantle was heavy.

I addressed the vet. "Let's say we do go to Gainesville and we find out Bear does have a brain tumor. Then what?"

"Well, one option could be surgery. But at his age, I wouldn't recommend it. The next option, which in my opinion would be the best for Bear, is medication, which could manage his seizures, hopefully minimize the frequency and severity of them."

"And if we don't go to Gainesville?"

"Then I would suggest we go ahead and start him on the medication to head off any future seizures."

I looked at each of the kids, then turned back to the vet and asked, "And what if we wait and see? What if we held off on the medication for now and wait to see if he actually has any more seizures?" I still wasn't completely on board this wasn't a one-off, some fluke occurrence. I looked at the kids and could see they felt the same way, as they nodded their heads in agreement. They liked this idea.

The vet looked resigned. "You can do that. But if he has another seizure, it could be worse than this first one. It could lead to irreparable neurological damage." He paused to let that sink in. But it couldn't penetrate our thick denial skin. We had already convinced ourselves Bear would be fine. We couldn't fathom any other possibility.

The vet breathed out a long sigh. "You can wait and see. But if Bear has another seizure, then you really need to bring him back in so we can get him started on the medication. In the meantime, I would recommend following up with your family vet."

∼

THE NEXT DAY WAS FRIDAY. All the kids were heading out of town to spend the weekend with their dad at his beach house, about thirty minutes north of my new home. I'd be on my own with Bear, who seemed to be doing okay in the light of day, slowly returning to his usual chipper self. I'd called our family vet, who was surprised to hear about the seizure and inquired if perhaps Bear had ingested anything unusual in the last few days (she knew her patient) that may have precipitated this. I liked her line of thinking, implying that maybe the seizure could be a random, isolated event.

That night, as I brushed my teeth before going to bed, both Bear and Skye in their crates for the night, I reflected on the past twenty-four hours, grateful that Bear seemed okay and growing in my confidence that the seizure was a fluke. I got under my covers, turned my lamp off, and settled in for a good night's rest.

I hadn't been asleep but thirty minutes, maybe forty, when I heard it. That same sound as the night before. Dread squeezed my chest as I turned my lamp on and looked over at the dogs' crates. There was Bear, in the thrall of another seizure, thrashing up against his crate.

Oh dear God in heaven above, help me. Help me help my Bear.

Not knowing what to do, and knowing I couldn't do anything for Bear until his seizure left him, and not wanting to feel so alone, I called Wilson.

Without preamble, I lurched right in. "He's having another seizure, Wils. What should I do? Take him back to the hospital? It's eleven o'clock at night. Do I take him back? Do I call them? Do I wait? Oh dear God. It wasn't a fluke, Wilson. It wasn't a fluke."

I could hear lots of noise in the background, a party going on. Then I heard a door slam and the unmistakable rumble of

Wilson's rusty blue truck starting up. Over the noise, I heard him say, "I'm coming, Mom. I'm coming."

"Wilson, you don't need to come all the way back down here." *Oh please, God, thank you. Thank you, thank you, thank you.* But I reiterated: "Wilson, you don't have to come. Just talk to me. Tell me what to do. Help me figure out what to do next."

"I'm coming, Mom. I'm on my way. I'm already out on A1A. Tell me what happened. When did it start? Is it still going on?" And he stayed on the phone with me until he pulled up in my driveway, got out of his truck, and walked through the door.

Bear staggered around like a drunk, weaving this way and that. He hardly registered Wilson's presence. Wilson called the animal hospital and spoke with the same vet we saw the night before. We were on board now with getting Bear on anti-seizure medication. The hard reality that something really was wrong with Bear had knocked denial's complacency right out of us. Since by now it was almost midnight, the vet suggested we could wait until the morning to bring Bear back in.

Wilson and I slept in the living room so we could keep an eye on Bear. We didn't want him to be confined to his crate and possibly injure himself if he had another seizure, so both dogs slept at our feet while we slept fitfully on the couches.

When we returned to the animal hospital early the next morning, the same vet was on duty.

Does he ever go home?

He told us Bear would need to stay at the hospital for the next twenty-four hours so they could administer the anti-seizure medication intravenously, get it established in his system, and watch for any serious side effects. Then Bear could start on the oral form of the med. The vet went over all the things that could go wrong and had us sign a paper about whether we wanted Bear resuscitated should he stop breathing. It was too much.

After we took care of the paperwork and said goodbye to Bear, we reluctantly walked out to the parking lot, not wanting to leave our dog behind. I had insisted on driving separately so Wilson could get back to his weekend with his dad and the other kids. When I reached out to hug him goodbye, he broke down in my arms. I held him as he cried.

I picked Bear up Sunday morning and was not prepared for what awaited me. Bear was achingly lethargic, moving like a sloth, his soulful brown eyes drooping—the antithesis of his personality. The staff said it was a side effect that could last several weeks until Bear's body became fully acclimated to the medication. I was given instructions to give him the medication every twelve hours. Not twice a day. Not maybe an hour earlier or an hour later here or there. Precisely. Every. Twelve. Hours. This was the best way, I was told, to keep the medication at a therapeutic level in his body, to keep the seizures at bay. Bear had received his first oral dose at six o'clock that morning, so his next dose would be due at six o'clock that night, and the next morning's dose at six, and so on.

Does this mean I have to wake up at six in the morning for the rest of Bear's life?

Just as this reality settled over me, they said if I wanted to adjust the timing of his dose, I would need to do so in the tiniest of increments, a few minutes each day.

It turned out that the next few days, I didn't have even the tiniest of increments to think about it. April came home from her dad's that evening, and in the midst of caring for Bear, we spent the next couple of days unpacking more boxes—finding places for all my books—so Bear (and Skye too) would have room to move around and be more comfortable in the new space.

On that Tuesday, eight days after I moved in, we began to hear talk about a hurricane that might be headed our way. Our area had not seen a hurricane in more than ten years. It had been so long that I had not seriously considered the likelihood of hurricanes when I bought my new house on the barrier island. Now it looked like a hurricane was coming this way and I was living on a spit of land less than half a mile wide between the Intracoastal Waterway and the Atlantic Ocean.

What was I thinking, moving up here, a breath away from the tumultuous surf?

April left for Argentina on Wednesday, and after I returned from dropping her off at the airport, I began prepping my house for the incoming storm—placing towels in the windowsills in case of leaks, getting things off the floor in case of flooding, bringing the patio furniture inside, gathering my important papers. Then I went to Publix to stock up on hurricane food and supplies: batteries, paper products, water, comfort snacks. Although it had been more than a decade since our last hurricane, I had lived in Florida long enough to know the drill.

But something new for me was living a stone's throw from the ocean and the necessity of hurricane shutters. We never had proper shutters for our family home on the mainland. Sometimes we—meaning, Jay—boarded up the east-facing windows when a hurricane was predicted to be dangerously strong. But most of the time, we didn't bother. That's because we were on the mainland and had the barrier island to protect us from the brunt of any storm. That's what barrier islands are for—to be a barrier.

What was I thinking, moving to a barrier island?

I remember the realtor mentioned hurricane shutters came with my new home, and I remember thinking at the time, in a distracted kind of way, *Oh, that's nice,* not really registering I may be required to employ them nine days after I moved in.

I came to find out there are different kinds of hurricane shutters. There are the electronic kind that are attached to the house above each window and, with a flip of a switch, roll down over the window, like a vertical accordion. Then there are the kind attached to each side of the window, similar to traditional cosmetic shutters, and manually pulled together, like a horizontal accordion, over the window. And then there are the kind I inherited with my new house. The least expensive and most complicated kind. Custom-made corrugated metal slats about twelve inches wide and the height of each window. The width of the window determines how many slats are needed.

My mind traveled back to when I first toured my home with Meredith and how we loved the light streaming in through all the windows. Now all I could see were *all the windows* that needed shuttering.

Meredith, Anthony, Wilson, and Wilson's three housemates came up that evening, and we all worked together to figure out which of the metal slats went on which windows (three to five slats to a window) as well as the three sets of sliding glass doors (six to eight slats per set) *and* three single doors that had full-length glass inserts (three slats each).

We located the box with the screws and wingnuts, and inside it we found a schematic of the house, with numbers written by each window and door. The slats were numbered as well, so we laid the slats out in the yard, in front of their corresponding windows and doors, then came up with a system for who held the slat in place, who screwed it in above and below the window, and who tightened it with the wing nut. Over and over and over again. Eventually, some time well after dark, we got the house secured. We celebrated with pizza and beer.

In the midst of all this, I gave Bear his meds every day at six in the morning and six in the evening, on the dot. He was still sluggish, adjusting to his new reality, but had not had any more seizures. I was grateful for that, though I longed for him to return to his old self.

Thursday morning, the authorities declared a mandatory evacuation of the barrier island. I would need to leave before they closed the bridge, which would happen once the winds reached forty miles per hour. Otherwise, I'd have to stay for the duration of the storm. I finished my preparations, then packed Skye and Bear, along with Bear's meds, all my important papers, and my hurricane supplies, into my little red station wagon and drove the seven miles back to town, over the bridge to the mainland, to hunker down at Wilson's house.

There had been some discussion about who I would stay with—Meredith and Anthony or Wilson. Meredith and Anthony's spacious house made more sense, since Wilson's house was full with three other guys living there, but Wilson said he wanted to help with the dogs. I knew he wanted Bear close to him, so I decided to stay with him.

When I arrived, I was surprised to see him and his housemates boarding up the windows.

"Do you think it's going to get that bad over here?" I hollered up to Wilson, who was standing on a ladder with a drill.

"They're now calling for a Cat 3 up this way, depending on how close to shore it comes," he yelled down from his perch.

"Wow." A Category 3 hurricane had a range of 111–129 mph winds closest to its eye, the center, but the wind field could extend hundreds of miles. I remember Hurricane Floyd back in '99 was more than five hundred miles across.

After drilling a screw into the plywood that his buddies held up, he continued, "Right now, it's a Cat 4 down in the Bahamas. With all my trees, I don't want to take any chances of flying debris smashing into my windows."

I looked up at the canopy of massive oaks in his yard. "Sounds wise to board up," I said, thinking of my little home facing the brunt of the storm. What if the surf surged right over it?

Bear and Skye and I slept in Wilson's bedroom that night while he slept on the couch in the living room. Around five the next morning, he came and roused me.

"It's starting to get rough out there," he said. "Winds are really picking up, and the rain is torrential. I think we should get the dogs out now. Then we'll have to keep them in until it passes."

We donned our rain jackets and galoshes and took the dogs out to do their business. Once we came back in and got ourselves and the dogs dried off, we made some coffee and tea and breakfast. I remembered to give Bear his anti-seizure medication. A few hours later, we lost power as the winds howled their fury around us. It wasn't until late in the day, when the hurricane pulled away from us, that we could finally venture outside with the dogs. Tree limbs were scattered everywhere, but no damage had been done to the house.

I was anxious to check on my home, but they weren't opening the bridge until the next morning. When I told Wilson I was going to head up there as soon as the bridge opened, he suggested maybe he and Anthony could take a ride up there first.

"I'm perfectly capable of tending to my home, Wilson," I retorted, feeling somewhat indignant.

"What if it's uninhabitable, Mom? What then? You can't be traipsing up there with the dogs, especially with Bear in his condition. Let Anthony and I drive up there and scope it out for you."

He had been in touch with his dad, whose beach house further up the coast had been inundated with three feet of water from the storm surge. Wilson had real concerns about my house.

I finally relented.

Once they arrived, they found both my fence gates torn off their hinges and gaping holes where the fence had been flattened in several places in the backyard, but the house was intact. I fared better than a lot of my neighbors, whose homes would need new roofs. We were all fortunate there was no water intrusion in any of our homes. In fact, there was no flooding anywhere in the neighborhood. I learned later that in our small area, A1A sat twelve feet above sea level, which is unusual. In many of the lower-lying coastal areas in our county, the storm surge had washed over A1A. About five miles north, the road had completely washed out, the asphalt broken into huge chunks by the rough sea.

The best news was I still had electricity. The utility lines in our neighborhood ran underground, so apparently I had never lost power. The kids came up to stay with me for a few days until their power was restored. Together, we took down my hurricane shutters and moved my patio furniture back outside. As we sat down on my lanai to take a break, we breathed a collective sigh of relief, knowing it could have been so much worse.

～

THREE MONTHS LATER, on a dreary Tuesday afternoon in mid-January, I found out my father had died. Out of the blue, my cousin texted me, saying she had just left my father's funeral and was headed to his burial, that he had finally succumbed to the pancreatic cancer after an eight-month battle.

I had no idea he had been sick.

She went on to say she knew no one wanted me to know, that they were keeping it a secret from me, but she thought I ought to know that my own father had passed away.

I was stunned. I sat down on my couch and kept staring at the message, reading it over and over again, trying to make some sense from it.

This isn't the way it was supposed to end.

In the early years after the estrangement, I had obsessed over it, imagining that one day, when he was sick and dying, he would send for me. Or someone would. Maybe the hospice chaplain would be the one to call and say my father was on his deathbed and wanted me to come so he could make amends. And I would have the freedom to say, "No, I'm not coming." Or maybe I would go. I didn't know. But what I did know was I would have the freedom to choose. The agency.

Eventually, I had stopped thinking about it. As the years went on, I stopped thinking about him.

I sat on my elephant-colored couch that Tuesday afternoon, trying to notice what I was feeling. Shock and surprise that he had been sick for *eight months*—plenty of time—and never sent for me. He really did carry it to his grave. He really did.

And then sadness. A deep sorrow that he would never acknowledge what he did. Underneath those feelings, I recognized the feeling of relief. He was finally gone.

Then I remembered it was Tuesday afternoon. The kids were coming that night for dinner, like they did every Tuesday night. I always made a home-cooked meal for them, had planned to make chicken pot pie that night, but now I didn't feel like cooking. I did feel like I wanted their company, though.

They knew my story. With the estrangement, it had become their story too, although it happened a long time ago. They were so young at the time. Wilson was only ten, Meredith eight, that summer I turned thirty-seven.

I texted them, asking if they would pick up some carryout.

Wilson, Meredith, and Anthony arrived that night with a huge bag from Outback. Once we sat down at the table with our food and I poured each of us a glass of wine, I told them about the death of my father, their grandfather.

"What I don't understand is why no one wanted me to know that he died," I said, "that they intentionally kept it from me."

"Sounds like maybe they were afraid you would show up at the funeral and tell the truth about him," said Meredith, slicing the brown loaf of dinner bread.

"When did he actually die?" asked Wilson as he cut into his Alice Springs chicken.

I pushed my pasta around my plate with my fork. "I don't know. I don't have any details, other than his funeral was today."

Meredith passed the bread to Anthony. After he took a slice and slathered it with whipped butter, he offered, "His obituary is probably online; we can google it."

Before I could respond, Meredith, a swift internet sleuth, had it pulled up on her phone. "He died three days ago," she said, skimming the obit. "But wait, look at this. This isn't right. This doesn't make sense."

"What? What? What is it?" I asked, my wine glass halfway to my mouth.

"We're all listed in the obituary. You, Dad, Me, Wilson, April."

"*What?*" I set the wine glass down, flabbergasted.

Meredith frowned at Anthony. "You're not there. Obviously, they didn't know we were married." Then she looked at me. "They also didn't know you and Dad are no longer together, Mom. They listed him as your husband."

I couldn't believe any of it. "Let me see that," I said, reaching for her phone.

There it was in black and white.

I took a big gulp of my Chardonnay.

"What kind of messed-up stuff is this," I said, "listing me and my family in the obituary but then making sure I knew nothing about his death or the funeral arrangements?"

Between mouthfuls of broccoli and chicken, Wilson said, "It's like they're trying to make it look like you're at fault, like you didn't even show up for your own dad's funeral."

They wanted to shame me.

I blew out a long breath. "That sounds just like them."

I watched Meredith dip one of her coconut shrimp in the marmalade, then take a bite of it. She chased it with a sip of wine, cleared her throat, and declared, "It's like I said before. They were afraid you would show up and tell the truth."

And I did already. I told the truth.

I nodded, looking at the three of them gathered around our old pine farm table, the same table we ate at when Meredith and Wilson were eight and ten years old.

This is what a family looks like.

"Thank you guys for coming tonight," I said. "Thank you for talking through this with me, helping me make some sense of it."

Anthony raised his glass to all of us and said, "A toast. Here's to a new way to be a family."

A month later, the day after Valentine's Day, my divorce was final.

~

I survived the hurricane. I survived the slow, sad decline of Bear's health—he never did fully recover—and his ensuing death a year later. I survived the death of my estranged father and the hard reality that he would never—not even on his deathbed—acknowledge his transgressions against me. I survived the gut-wrenching divorce process that lasted over a year and, in its wake, the long trajectory toward healing.

The day I saved the drowning armadillo, I had remembered I could tackle hard things and survive. I had learned I didn't need to passively wait around for someone to rescue me, that I had the resourcefulness and resilience to tackle hard things all on my own.

What I hadn't realized that day was that I had not saved the armadillo *all on my own.* The armadillo, himself, was actively engaged in his own survival, furiously swimming laps around the perimeter of that pool, trying to find a way out. But as hard as he tried, he still needed help.

I was learning it doesn't have to be one or the other: being passively rescued or doing it all on my own. I was learning I could tackle hard things *and* I could accept help. Even ask for it. I was learning I could count on my children. And they could count on me. I was learning about the changing shape of my family and that although I was no longer a wife, I was still very much a mother. My children were still my children. We were still a family.

We were learning together how to live into the new shape of our family, how to be a family in a new way.

Chapter 7

Sanctuary by the Sea

Thread of Light: Grieve your losses and take time to heal

Once I had the chance to settle in, I discovered my new home in my new neighborhood nestled between the river and the sea was actually a shelter from the storm. I found it to be a safe place for me, a place away from all the eyes—pitying, prying, assessing, avoiding eyes—of those who wondered what had happened to a seemingly happy marriage. I experienced none of that from my new neighbors, which felt so refreshing. The week after the hurricane, when I encountered several women at our communal mailboxes and we introduced ourselves, I briefly mentioned I was going through a divorce and had moved up here from town. They nodded like they understood. They didn't prod or poke or exclaim or exhort. They simply gave me space without ignoring me.

Anne and Emma, both exercise enthusiasts, invited me to come along on their daily four-mile walks. Dale, whom I met when she was out walking her dog and I was walking Skye, would stop and chat for a few minutes when we passed each other on the road. I learned she had been divorced more than twenty years and never remarried, and it gave me a tiny glimpse into how life might one day become full again without a husband. Dalia, the creator and keeper of the laminated list of neighbors and their contact information, asked if I'd like to be included. When I said yes, she updated and distributed new copies to the neighborhood.

Wayne and Carol, my neighbors across the street who were usually in their yard planting flowers or trimming hedges, would stop their work to say hi when they saw me walk by. Carol brought over homemade cookies at Christmas, and Wayne captured the black snake that kept showing up in my backyard, relocating it to the wildlife sanctuary he and Carol had cultivated at the back of their property. When another snake showed up, he'd be right over to do it again.

And there were others too. Ginger, Joan, and Tim and Carol on the next street over; Pam and Christine down in the cul-de-sac. There were no big social gatherings, no obligatory meetups. No one showed up at the door unannounced. There was tremendous respect for one another's privacy, and yet there was an openness, a generosity of spirit without being intrusive, when neighbors saw one another on the street. No one was ever too busy to slow down and catch up with another's day.

Aside from my kids, who came up for Tuesday night dinners, I seldom had visitors from town. I had lost most of my friends in the divorce; they had been the wives of the men in my husband's circle of friends, and when I no longer belonged to him, they no longer bothered with me.

Maggie Smith, in her memoir *You Could Make This Place Beautiful*, which chronicles her divorce experience, talks about how so much in her life stayed the same post-divorce: same house, same neighbors, same friends, same family.[1] It reminded me how so much for me did *not* stay the same. It reminded me of all the losses embedded in my divorce, including the loss of my friends and my husband's entire extended family, all sixteen of them.

Poof. Gone.

Several years ago, I attended a workshop by spiritual director Daniele Evans.[2] She talked about when we have experienced an unexpected event or situation that shakes us to our core, it can feel like we've entered into a kind of wilderness—a place where we no longer have a sense of belonging, where we no longer feel we have a space that is ours to inhabit. We are disoriented and left with feelings of anxiety, fear, and shame. We are in the wilderness.

Daniele offered two invitations for navigating our wilderness seasons. The first is the invitation of insulation. Rather than feeling like we are isolating ourselves when we choose to distance ourselves from those who have wounded us, she asked us to consider what it might look like to see this time as insulating ourselves instead. Putting our energy toward providing care for ourselves rather than toward getting away. It's about saying, "This is the new space I need," rather than saying, "That is the old space I need to get away from."

That is what that sliver of land between the river and the sea provided for me during my wilderness season: a place of insulation, where I could tend to my wounds without worrying about getting wounded further. A place to rest, to catch my breath. I began a practice of walking to the river in the evenings to watch the sunset. When the moon was full, I'd walk to the ocean to see it rise over that vast body of water. These practices soothed my weary soul.

My neighbors helped provide a space of insulation too. They were like a gentle, steady rain upon the hardness of a rock, the armor of my heart, slowly allowing me to feel like I could let my guard down, that I didn't have to stay closed up tight to protect my wounds. I could let them breathe.

The second invitation Daniele offered in her workshop was the invitation to be proactive about creating a space for ourselves in the wilderness. She decreed that we get to decide how we will respond to what has happened to us. We can ask ourselves, *What do I need so I can tend to my sorrow? How can I begin to pay attention to my emotional, spiritual, mental, and physical well-being and nurture myself back to health?*

That is what my home provided for me during my wilderness season: a space where I could be proactive about healing. I sat on my back lanai in the tranquility of my secluded backyard, Bear and Skye lounging nearby, and let the soothing sound of the surf wash over my sorrow. I sobbed and sobbed and sobbed. I journaled and journaled and journaled. And I sobbed some more. Every morning, a menagerie of birds lined up along the back fence line and chirped their melodies of solace to my sore, spent soul.

As author Kathy Swaar says in her book *Fines Lines: Walking the Labyrinth of Grief and Loss*, it was a time to "face, name, own, and articulate" all the losses I had experienced.[3] Family members who no longer thought I was family. Friends who no longer wanted to be friends. The man I once loved—the *only* man I ever loved—who had become a stranger. Loss of a shared history. Loss of a shared future. Loss of being someone else's most important person. My identity as a wife. My status as a married woman. The home that raised my children and gave them roots. Loss of my nuclear family unit. Loss of the narrative of my life. Loss of my sense of self.

In the state of Florida, the official legal terminology for a marital divorce is *dissolution of marriage*. To divorce means to separate, to sever or divide into separate parts. To dissolve means to disperse, to evaporate or vanish.

Poof. Gone.

Daniele said that being proactive about creating a space for ourselves to heal is not only about grieving all we have lost; it is also a time to look around and notice what is left. To wonder what might be nurtured in the space created by absence.

How do you nurture something when there is nothing left?

My therapist suggested I start with a gratitude practice, writing down three things I was grateful for each day. It felt like such a cliché. Swallowed up by all my loss, gratitude was not on my radar, and at first I stubbornly opposed the idea. I felt like there was nothing to be grateful for. And I certainly didn't want to have to entertain the notion of being grateful for all that had happened to me, to offer up some kind of obligatory thanksgiving, when deep down I wasn't grateful at all. No thank you.

But then I read about Facebook executive Sheryl Sandberg's daily practice of writing down three things she did well each day, a practice she implemented in the months after her husband's death. She said sometimes the only thing she could think of that she did well that day was make a cup of tea.[4] For me, thinking about things I did well only magnified my shortcomings, so that practice wasn't going to work for me. But reading about her cup of tea helped me realize maybe I *could* start small with a gratitude practice, paying attention to the simplest of things and being honest about it. I was grateful for the sound of the surf. I was grateful for the birds. I was grateful for my morning cup of tea while I cried.

Taking the time to reflect on what I was truly grateful for each day didn't take away or submerge my grief. But it did shift my focus, even if only for a few moments each day, and it helped me to see that although it *felt* like my grief took up the whole of my life, that wasn't actually true.

In addition to my gratitude practice, I set an intention to seek out connection each day, however brief or small. This practice came about because one day I realized I had not spoken to another soul all day—well, other than Bear and Skye. That was a lonely, lonely feeling. My therapist thought I should join a civic organization or a bowling league. I rolled my eyes when she said this. The last thing I wanted to do was be forced into mingling with strangers, making small talk. But I also knew I needed to make an effort not to continue to wallow in my own sea of grief.

So, alongside my list of gratitude each day, I started writing down connections that occurred, both those that happened naturally and those I intentionally sought out. Waving to a neighbor down the block, smiling at the postal carrier as I picked up my mail, texting one of my kids to say good morning. It wasn't much to start with, but seeking out and naming my connections each day helped me remember I wasn't alone on some random raft of driftwood, floating aimlessly. Even if I didn't feel like it, I was part of an interrelated web of life.

Jan Richardson, in her 2017 Women's Christmas retreat, titled "Walking the Way of Hope," writes, "Hope is what happens when we dare to sit with what has shattered, to weep over the wreckage, and to begin to imagine how the pieces could connect in a new way."[5] Both these practices of gratitude and connection became a way for me to ever so slowly begin to imagine that the pieces of my life could one day come together in a new way. They became a portal for hope to find a way back into my heart.

And I began writing again. Before the separation, I had worked on a set of essays about my time as a university chaplain, exploring a myriad of interactions I had with students, staff, and faculty that stayed with me long after I left my position. I wanted to compile these stories in some way but didn't have a clue how to develop them into a book-length manuscript.

To help me find my footing, I scheduled a consultation with Christianne Squires, a book editor and spiritual director who helped writers "birth their book without losing their soul." [6] She sounded like a godsend, but I wasn't sure I was ready to begin working with her. Would she even consider working with me? I felt like I had already lost my soul and needed to try and find it before immersing myself back into my writing vocation. Christianne encouraged me to move forward, suggesting that getting back to my writing might contribute to my healing. And it did.

The process of writing led me back to the core of who I am. It honored my introverted, introspective self. It affirmed my inquisitive, imaginative nature. It nurtured my creative capabilities. And it helped me find my voice again and claim how I am called to bear light in the world.

I was surprised to discover how spacious it felt to delve into a writing routine in my new life. There was the space of my home, uncluttered by anyone else's presence. There was the space in my life, with no one else's schedule to consider. And there was a new spaciousness in my spirit, not being constrained by someone else's prescription of how we should live our shared lives or of how I needed to conform to fit into their life. It created a space that allowed my true self to take root, to unfurl, to stretch, to reach toward light. All this space gave me courage to listen more deeply to my own story and convey my experiences more authentically through my writing.

With the guidance and companionship of Christianne, I discerned an intriguing theme emerging in my chaplaincy stories. My book wanted to be about the common spaces between us and how giving one another the space we need helps us to recognize, honor, and nurture the good in one another, and in ourselves too. Sometimes this means paying attention to the worthiness of our inner voice. Sometimes it means suspending judgment, both with others and ourselves. Sometimes it is about creating a safe space for those who embody different values than we do.

Writing my book in the new spaciousness of my spirit, in the airiness of my home located within the gentle benevolence of my neighborhood and situated on the lovely sliver of land between the river and the sea—it gave new energy to my soul and new meaning to my life.

As my book took shape and I pondered my publishing options, Christianne introduced me to the Bookwifery Collective, a small group of writers also working with her to birth books. We met weekly via Zoom to reflect on our writing journeys and encourage one another. Over time we became friends and began sharing our lives beyond our creative endeavors. This eventually led me to a new online community, also led by Christianne, called the Light House, "a spiritual home for contemplative women bearing light in big and small ways."[7] It indeed became a spiritual home for me, filled with kindred spirits.

As all this unfolded over my years in the wilderness, I came to recognize just how much had been nurtured in the space created by absence. My own sense of self-worth. My calling. New friends. A new community. A new book birthed into the world. My light-filled home and my gracious neighbors and my remote little neighborhood between the river and the sea had given me the space I needed to grieve and the space I needed to heal. It was the space I needed to imagine a new future for myself and the space to begin living into that future.

I thought I would stay there forever.

But then, in my fifth year there, I sensed a nudge to return back to town. I drove to Wilson's house more often, now that

Baby Charlotte had been born and I took care of her every Wednesday morning. April had returned from Argentina and bought a home in town; I'd probably see her more often if I moved back. Meredith and Anthony had moved to another city a few years ago for Ant's job, but now they had Baby Isla and came back often to visit. They usually stayed with Jay, who had sold the beach house and bought a house in town a year earlier, because his house was "so conveniently located," they said. As a result, I didn't see them as much as I wanted when they were in town. Maybe if I moved back, they could start staying with me?

But I also resisted the nudge. I loved my Heron Dunes home. I loved my neighborhood. I loved my neighbors. All of it was my sanctuary, my cocoon. I didn't want to give it up. And besides, what if I moved back and my kids didn't hang out with me as much as I would like? What then? They had their own lives. I didn't want to move back in hopes of what they might do.

What if you moved back for your own sake?

This question surprised me. I knew it came from that voice that kept nudging me, kept invading my thoughts.

It said, "You could move back for your own sake, you know. No more endless driving up and down A1A. No more trying to get all your errands and appointments synchronized for Wednesday afternoons, when you're in town. Imagine the freedom of choosing any day you want to go to Publix or Walgreens or the shops. It wouldn't interfere with your writing work; in fact, you could bop over to Starbucks in less than five minutes if you felt inspired to work there that day. It would be like it used to be when you lived in the center of town for twenty-five years, connected to everything and everyone. You would be home."

This reminded me why I left the year of the divorce. I

didn't want to be connected to everything and everyone anymore. I didn't want to run into people who wondered what went wrong in my marriage, why I sold the house, why I was moving away. Why would I want to go back to that?

The nudging voice replied, "That was five years ago! People have moved on. *You* have moved on."

Well. That was certainly something to think about. I *had* moved on. I was not the same person who left town five years ago. I'd become strong in these intervening years. And brave. I was learning how to live an undivided life. More grounded. Centered. I was becoming more at home in my own being.

That nudging voice may be on to something.

I let myself consider what it might feel like to live back in town again, connected in a different way than before.

That's when I realized that the nudge to move back was also a whisper in my ear that my sanctuary by the sea well north of town had served its purpose. It had saved me.

It was time to return home.

Chapter 8

Two Little Lights

Thread of Light: Let joy woo you

It was mid-December. The stockings had been hung for a week or so, and I swore I could hear them whisper their stories to me. They whispered about the new life I'd grown over the past four years, since I'd moved to Heron Dunes Drive.

Meredith, Anthony, and Wilson's stockings reminded me of the first Christmas in my new home, when they came to help me decorate the tree and sort through thirty years of ornaments, crying and laughing and loving me through it.

Bear and Skye's stockings, adorned with crocheted brown and black Labs, whispered to me too. Although they had both passed away since I moved to Heron Dunes, I still wanted to honor their memory by hanging their stockings. Grief mixed with gratitude as I remembered my beloved companions and all they had accompanied me through.

On each side of April's stocking hung a smaller stocking for each of her cats. About a year after I moved into the house, she had returned permanently from her life in Argentina, bringing two kittens, Potro and Tabby, home with her. Initially, she split her time between her dad and me, staying a few weeks with one of us, then with the other. My mama heart rested easier with her near.

My new(ish) puppy, River, had her own stocking too. She was a rascal from the first day home, wild and rowdy, even by Labrador puppy standards. I had misgivings I had chosen the wrong puppy. But over time—she was two that Christmas— she'd let me tame some of her wildness, and some of her wildness livened up my subdued nature.

Next to Wilson's stocking hung a new stocking, the stocking of his lovely bride, Bridget. They had married earlier that year in a ceremony I was honored to officiate. It was such a pleasure welcoming her into our family and watching how she brought out the best in my son.

My own stocking whispered its story, too, how it came into my life that first Christmas in that home. It hadn't taken long for me to realize my old stocking, the one that had been part of another life for more than three decades, the stocking my former husband had faithfully filled with trinkets and treasures for so many years, needed to be replaced. It carried too many memories that weighed me down. This new stocking, clothed with sprouts of green leaves and berries, spoke a story of growth, reminding me how far I'd traveled from the time grief had swallowed my hope, when I was encompassed by all I had lost.

Two additional stockings hung from the shelf that year, whispering stories to me. That summer, two months apart, two precious babies were born into our family, one belonging to Meredith and Anthony, and one belonging to Wilson and Bridget. I became a nana—and a joy I didn't know could be part of my constitution woke up in my heart.

Joy and I had never really been friends. As an emotion, I thought her overrated. She always seemed fleeting to me, here for a moment in time, like a guest who shows up on special occasions and then departs as soon as the festivities are over.

She showed up when each of my kids was born. Joy pervaded the room—and my heart—as I first laid eyes on each of my children, as I held them in my arms, as I pored over their features, smitten with them already. Others shared in our joy, too, and reflected our joy by their gifts of balloons and flowers and crocheted baby blankets. But then reality set in with diapers, feedings, cracked nipples, and sleepless nights. Exhaustion and overwhelm took over, and joy went off to find someone else to hang out with.

She also showed up when each of them graduated from high school. It was such a joyous time, celebrating all they had accomplished and the bright futures that lay ahead. Joy lingered long into the summer those years. But then she moved on as they matriculated to college, when worry and fear came to be my friends and joy felt outnumbered.

Joy never seemed dependable to me. Looking back over the years, though, I wonder if maybe I was the one who wasn't dependable. Maybe joy wanted to be lifelong friends but it felt one-sided. I don't remember seeking her out; I didn't encourage her. I was more like the character Michael in the novel *You Are Here*, who "realised he had accidentally been lulled into enjoying himself."[1] I didn't go looking for joy, and when other emotions showed up in my life, I let them take up all the space.

Maybe it was a coping mechanism. Maybe it was habit. Maybe I was afraid of her. Maybe I just didn't understand her. Maybe I thought she'd be too disruptive, too much of an antidote to sadness, my true-blue friend. Maybe I thought she'd try and take over my sadness, crowd him out, act like he wasn't there, act like what had caused him to show up in the first place didn't matter. And that didn't seem right. I was loyal to my sadness because he bore witness to the truth.

Besides, it had always bothered me the way some people talked about joy. "Be joyful!" they commanded, like it was something I could choose to put on, to wear, like a party hat. Even worse were those who insisted joy was like an inner light that never dimmed, as long as you kept it lit. It sounded exhausting. With my tendency toward a melancholy disposition, I preferred contentment instead, a friendship I felt could be sustained over the long haul. Why did I need joy? I was moving forward with my quiet, contemplative life. I was moving in the direction of inner peace. I was learning to be content. It was enough.

But then these two little lights came into the world and into my life, and joy came alive in my heart.

At first I thought my granddaughters had brought the joy to me. But then I realized that wasn't quite the whole story. What they had done was *spark* the joy that lay latent, waiting, within me.

Unfamiliar as I was with joy, the photos gave me the first inkling she had made herself at home, sitting in my heart and pouring herself a cup of tea while her partner, delight, helped herself to my stash of chocolate. I almost didn't recognize myself in those early pictures. When had I last seen my smile reach my eyes? Radiate my countenance? These photos were of no special occasion, no festivities, but the transformation of my face said it all: joy and delight had moved in, taking up residence in my melancholy heart with my old friend contentment and my new nana self.

How did it happen, exactly?

I think, first, the presence of my grandbabies ushered me

into the realm of awe and wonder. Just looking at these creatures, so delicately made from the flesh of my own children—
my *own* flesh—left me mesmerized. There had not been much
awe and wonder in my life since the divorce, and maybe not
much before that either.

Second, their presence invited me to move from caution to
curiosity. The divorce had left me so inhibited that I wasn't
even aware how much I restrained myself, held myself in
check, guarded my heart from any potential further wounding.
But when these two babies showed up, I was so curious about
them that I forgot to be cautious. And of course, I witnessed
their lack of inhibition, their spontaneity, their curiosity about
everything, and it became contagious.

Third, I was taken aback by delight. These babies had
already captured my delight in them, but then I became
cognizant that *they* also delighted in *me*. It had been a long time
since I felt like someone delighted in my presence—in me
simply being who I am, without having to keep my guard up or
make myself small or put on a facade. These babies delighted in
the real me. It was like they saw me at the core of who I am and
loved it, clapping their little hands in delight when I walked
into the room.

All of this—the awe and wonder, the movement from
caution to curiosity, the delight—breathed new life into me. I
was like Lazarus, loosening up the grave clothes I had wrapped
tightly around myself. It kindled something within me that was
dormant. Something I would have said before had lain down
and died within me. But now it was alive, the sleeping ash
having been breathed upon and fanned into existence. Joy was
awake in my heart.

I've learned a few things about her. I've realized joy is not
something that has to be constantly sustained within us. That
would be exhausting. And although she doesn't have to rely on

external circumstances, she certainly can—and often will—be ignited by them. And that's a good thing. I've learned it's about recognizing she's there and then discovering the myriad ways she might choose to wake up within us.

I've also learned joy and sorrow can be held together. I didn't have to wait until I stopped grieving to let joy in. Maggie Smith, in her book *Keep Moving*, writes, "Do not turn away joy —even if it arrives at an inconvenient time, even if you think you should be grieving, even if you think it's 'too soon.'"[2] I've learned joy can touch, bump up against, be held in tension with, even soften the hard things going on in my life.

And actually, when I look back at the Christmas stockings and the stories they whispered to me, I can see how she was there in some of those hard things. She showed up that night Wilson, Meredith, and Anthony helped me decorate the tree. Of course, decorating a Christmas tree should be a joyful event, but we all knew it would be hard, the first Christmas on my own, especially because no one had gone through the Christmas decorations since the previous year.

Back before we sold the family home, when we decided who got what, it had not occurred to Jay or me that perhaps the Christmas boxes in the attic should be sorted through, that we should divvy up the contents into piles the way we had done with the furniture and books and knickknacks. Neither of us thought about it. And so, on moving day, those boxes got packed into my moving van, none of the contents disturbed from the previous Christmas—the final Christmas of our marriage—when they were packed away.

You can imagine the grief waiting for us as the kids and I opened the boxes, as we took out the stockings and unwrapped the ornaments. The oval ornament inscribed with "Our First Year Together." The "My Kind of Town" ornament with an etching of the Chicago skyline, from our early married years there. The ornaments Jay and I bought together on our travels to Amelia Island, the Bahamas, Napa Valley. The ones we had given one another to commemorate another year shared together. All mixed in with the numerous ornaments we had given the kids during their childhood.

More than thirty years of memories came flooding back as the kids and I sorted through all those ornaments that told the story of my married life, our family life. We cried, and we laughed, and we loved one another through it. I was grateful for their presence with me that night, grateful for our present life together, even as I grieved that Christmas would never be the same again. Joy was in the room that night. In the cloak of connection, she showed up, even in the midst of grief.

Ross Gay, author of *Inciting Joy*, speaks to the deep essence of joy that shows up in the midst of grief when he asks, "What if joy is not only entangled with pain, or suffering, or sorrow, but is also what emerges from how we care for each other *through* those things?"[3] This is what I experienced that night, decorating the tree with Wilson, Meredith, and Anthony.

Gay's words help me to see, too, how joy was present in the belovedness of Bear and Skye in their last years with just me. They had been the quintessential family dogs, part of my previous life, and at times I felt they were all I had left to carry with me as I journeyed into the unknown. There were count- less nights I cried into their necks, each of them comforting me in their own way. I see now how joy was immersed in the bond I had with them, in the devoted comfort and care we gave one another. Joy doesn't always have to be the party animal, the social director on the cruise ship. She can read the room and be malleable to suit the situation. But she's still there.

And of course, I can now see how joy showed up with the new puppy, River, like she had snuck into the car when we drove home that first time, hiding herself deep within River's fur, a stowaway. River was not at all what I had in mind when I made the decision to bring a puppy home not quite a year after Bear died. Headstrong at eight weeks, stubborn and strong-willed, she wore me out. I had not thought through how hard it would be to raise a puppy on my own—so different from raising Bear and Skye within the context of our family. But worst of all, in those early months, she reminded me of my ex: I couldn't make her do what I wanted her to do, and I couldn't keep her from doing what I didn't want her to do. She really drained my spirit, and I wasn't sure we would still be together two years down the road.

I say River was wild, rowdy, and headstrong. And that is true. But maybe she was also exuberant with the joy of living and she couldn't contain it. Maybe it burst her seams. For my part, I can see how I wanted to snuff that joy right out of her. I wanted her to be staid, calm, compliant. But what happened instead, I think, was that her joy infected me. Like a flea, joy jumped right off River and latched herself onto me, seeping in. Even in the midst of my uptight attitude, joy found a way in. And when I let joy have a little wiggle room, an interesting thing happened. River began to settle down. Settle in. Settle into herself. Settle into life with me. And I settled down too. We found a way to abide together in mutual respect and love.

I can see how joy showed up in my new stocking, too, clothed with sprouts of green leaves and berries, a story of growth, a story of hope being nurtured in the midst of all the sadness. I see how hope made room for joy.

All this helped me realize there are nuances to joy, that other emotions, other states of being, can be part of joy too. Joy has precursors that ready us for her arrival. When I look back at April's permanent return from Argentina, joy was present in the deep sense of peace I felt in having her near once again, in the cherishing of our time together, in the deepening of our connection. Joy was present in the welcoming of Bridget into our family and my sense of gratitude in knowing my son had found his soulmate. I can even see how joy is cousin to my old friend contentment; they carry similar DNA.

Once my grandbabies were born and I began to understand joy, once I realized I didn't need to be afraid of her, that she wasn't trying to take away or crowd out or cover over my beloved other emotions, once I knew what she looked like and that she didn't have to look a specific way all the time—she might show up wearing different clothes, new hairstyles, sometimes with glasses, sometimes not—I could see how she wooed me well before I was aware enough to care.

She kept showing up for me, over and over again. And she keeps showing up. When I welcome her in, she bestows upon me a full-bodied feeling of fullness, enriching my life with a deep, layered texture of meaning, of well-being.

Chapter 9

The Lilly Beach Towel

Thread of Light: Make room for your younger selves

Every year I vacation on Amelia Island, off the coast of Jacksonville, Florida. I discovered the island when April was just a year old and Meredith and Wilson were three and five. The kids and I had tagged along with Jay for a conference he had there, located at the Ritz-Carlton resort. We fell in love with the island and the resort, so when our anniversary came around the following spring and we wanted to get away without the kids, Jay and I decided the Ritz on Amelia Island was the perfect place to celebrate. It became an anniversary tradition we continued the next twenty years.

As the kids became teenagers, I imagined how nice it might be to start a tradition of a long family weekend on Amelia Island, maybe renting a house or a condo—not in lieu of our anniversary weekend, but in addition to it. I wanted them to experience the island. I wanted them to fall in love with it the way I had. We could go around my birthday at the end of July, a time of togetherness before everyone went back to school in August.

When I brought the idea up with Jay, he nixed it, saying it wasn't in the budget for us all to stay at the Ritz. Before I could offer the suggestion of other accommodations, he finished with, "And *really*, could you imagine coming up here and not staying at the Ritz?"

Yes, yes I could.

But I never could get him on board with my vision.

So, years later, when the kids were in their twenties and I found myself in the middle of the muck of the divorce process and wanted to get away from it all, I remembered my longing for a family weekend on Amelia Island.

Would my grown-up kids be interested in going away with just me?

This was two months before I moved to Heron Dunes, a month before I saved the drowning armadillo. The kids spent almost every weekend with their dad at his beach house. It was a party place, and he was the "party parent."

Would they even consider vacationing with me?

I finally worked up the courage to ask each of them. I knew it wasn't going to work for April, down in Argentina, who would be coming home in September to help with my move. But I was relieved and excited when the others said yes.

So Wilson, Meredith, her new husband, Anthony, and I went up for three nights over my birthday weekend that summer. We rented a small, two-bedroom, weathered townhome right on the beach; I was in the primary bedroom, and the kids shared the other room, the one with three twin beds. My bedroom had a balcony that overlooked the ocean, just beyond the dunes. I remember that first night, looking out at the black sky radiant with stars and a full moon rising. I could taste the saltiness of the surf coming in on the breeze. I felt so close to the dunes and to the sea, to the energy of creation.

It took me back to a memory of going on a trip with Jay and some friends before we were married. We were in our late teens and had driven from our summer jobs on the farm in Maryland down to the Outer Banks of North Carolina, camping in a tent at an RV park steps from the beach. We loved the laid-back nature of it all: sleeping in the open air with the surf singing its lullaby, the sunrise our alarm clock, the wind in our hair, the spray of the salty sea on our faces. I remember thinking at the time, *This is all we need.*

As I stood on my balcony, fiddling with the diamond band I still wore on my left ring finger (I told myself I'd know when it was time to take it off), I wondered how we had moved so far from those early days, when all we wanted was a simple lifestyle.

I had fretted about how I might feel going back to the island where I celebrated my wedding anniversary for twenty years. But that first night, standing on my balcony under the canopy of stars, I felt at peace. I was free now to create my own kind of vacation with my children and my own kind of relationship with this island.

On our second night there, Meredith and Anthony made salmon for dinner, and it was scrumptious—though they had grossly overestimated how much salmon was needed to feed the four of us. There was *way too much* left over. Meredith came up with the idea to make salmon dip as an appetizer the next evening. That was the night we started a conversation about future vacations.

Wilson said, "We should do this next summer," as he scooped some salmon dip onto his club cracker.

Meredith, in between bites, added, "I could see us doing this *every* summer."

My heart swelled.

We all looked at Anthony, his mouth stuffed with salmon dip, who responded, "I'm in, as long as we have a salmon night *and* a salmon dip appetizer night!"

The second year, we discovered the North End of the island, where many of the old beach cottages and cabins date back a hundred years or more. I fell in love with the area up on this part of the island. It felt like Old Florida, before development took over, when the dunes flourished with sea oats rather than seawalls and views of the ocean weren't obstructed by high-rise hotels and condos.

That summer, we rented a cozy, three-bedroom cottage named Good Knight's Rest, located on a dirt road in front of the beach. April joined us, as did Bear and Skye. The kitchen wasn't much more than a lean-to at the back of the house, incredibly outdated with no dishwasher, and the bedrooms were so small that Wilson was relegated to the foldout couch. But the dining and living spaces provided plenty of room to gather for meals and lounge around after our days at the beach. At night we spent hours playing the game Heads Up and laughing our heads off (April was the "rhyme time" champ). In addition to our salmon night (*and* salmon dip appetizer night!), we inaugurated our first annual steak night, grilling out on the small charcoal grill that came with the cottage. Even though there were some inconveniences, we loved the quaintness of Good Knight's Rest and its proximity to the beach, so we stayed there the next year as well.

The year after that, with Wilson's sweetheart, Bridget, joining us, we rented a larger three-bedroom home. Bell's Retreat was further north than Good Knight's Rest, on the beach but also close to the woods of Fort Clinch State Park. Almost every evening, we encountered deer running through the dunes at twilight. We were mesmerized by the grace and agility of these beautiful creatures and delighted in watching them frolic together. It was so peaceful and serene with the deer, the dunes, and the sea right out our back door.

That was also the year Meredith gave me a beach towel for my birthday. It was a Lilly Pulitzer destination towel, with "Amelia Island, Florida" written in script across the top. In Lilly's signature vivid colors, the towel was full of palm trees and glittering ocean waves. I loved it. But as I held it up, I noticed that right in the middle of the towel was an image of a resort. It was the Ritz. The same Ritz-Carlton where we had celebrated our anniversary for twenty years. My heart sank. I knew I couldn't use this towel. Every time I looked at it, I would be reminded of all I had lost.

The next day, I decided to gift the towel back to Meredith. Surely she would understand I couldn't use this towel with the Ritz right in the middle of it. When we had a moment alone, I handed her the towel and tried to explain how I felt.

She waited patiently for me to finish, then said, "You know, Mom, the Ritz and all those years with Dad is part of what made you fall in love with this island. Those were good memories, even if they're hard for you to recall right now. And now you're making new memories here, with us. Maybe this towel can become a reminder for you of the new memories."

I just stared at her as she gently handed the towel back to me and walked away.

Huh.

What could I do but start using the towel?

We loved Bell's Retreat and returned the following year, but with Baby Isla and Baby Charlotte born that summer, we moved our vacation from July to October. We loved the more moderate temperatures of autumn, so this became the new time for our annual getaway. That year, we stayed an entire week, rather than a long weekend. I think we all could see the vision of how this vacation time could create a lifelong bond for these little cousins.

Bell's Retreat felt a little tight with the addition of two babies, so the next year we found a spacious log cabin to rent. We had so much fun seeing the beach through the eyes of Isla and Charlotte as they toddled around, exploring that vast playground filled with seashells, sand crabs, and tidal pools.

The year after that, the kids wanted to try a different location. Not just a different house, but a different island entirely, all the way across the state to the Gulf, to Anna Maria Island. Initially, I was disappointed to diverge from Amelia Island, not only because I loved the area but also because I loved the idea of going back to the same place every year; I felt like it contributed to the memory making. I also recognized in myself a niggling fear that this was the beginning of the slippery slope of losing agency over my kind of vacation. Would the kids want to go somewhere different every year and I would end up feeling like I was tagging along, no longer having a say in our annual time away?

I wanted to be a good sport, and I didn't want to become ingrained in needing our time together to look a specific way, so I went along with their desire—and I ended up loving Anna Maria Island. It wasn't Amelia Island, but it was still quaint and laid-back. More importantly, I realized what really mattered was not so much where we vacationed, but that we were vacationing together. I wanted this annual time away with my children and grandchildren to be the focus.

Remarkably, while our time in Anna Maria helped me see I didn't need our vacation to be tied to the same location each year, it helped the kids see that going back to the same place could be significant, watching their children experience the same place in different ways as they grew. I was elated when they agreed that, although Anna Maria Island held its own beauty and charm, they wanted Amelia Island to be our yearly vacation destination.

That was also the year the kids dubbed our annual time away "Nana's Family Vacay." And with a third grandchild, Baby Elizabeth, joining us that year, the name felt like the perfect fit. Like a warm embrace. It was my vacation *and* it had become my family's vacation. It was *our* vacation.

THE FOLLOWING YEAR, back on Amelia Island, it was difficult to find a home big enough to accommodate all of us, as Baby Harlynne and Baby James joined us that year (*five* grandchildren!). We found a few homes on the North End, but we decided to go with a home on the South End because it was the largest. Since it was offseason, it fit within our budget. A beautiful home, Mermaid Castle stood four stories tall, with multiple balconies and porches—plenty of room for everyone to spread out. But by the end of our stay, I wondered if it was too much space. It lacked the coziness I had come to look forward to when we gathered. And it felt a little too . . . well . . . ritzy.

The next year, we returned to our July vacation time since Isla and Charlotte were growing closer to school age. Summer was prime vacation time on the island, and Mermaid Castle's rental fee reflected that, putting it way over our budget. So we returned to the North End, where we found a more affordable option.

It felt like the summer vacations of those early years at Good Knight's Rest, where we loved making memories in the quaint simplicity of an old cottage on the dirt road that time forgot. The home we rented, Crump Sandcastle, was definitely more snug than Mermaid Castle, but it was a cozy snug. And overlooking the ocean was a spacious screened porch with two old-timey wooden double swings facing each other. It was the perfect spot for leisurely visiting with one another while the grands played underfoot. With the salt air coming in on the sea breeze, I felt blissfully suspended in time on that old Florida coast.

THAT FIRST YEAR, the year of the divorce, when I longed for a few days away with my kids on Amelia Island, I never could have imagined it would blossom into such a beloved tradition, the highlight of my year with my family.

I'm still using the beach towel Meredith gave me, the one with the Ritz-Carlton resort on it, surrounded by palm trees and ocean waves. She was right. When I look at that towel now, I'm filled with memories of these family vacations with my children and grandchildren. The Ritz is still there, but it doesn't feel as prominent as it did when Meredith first gave me the towel. Actually, it's hard for me to believe I once thought it stood out on the towel, because now it feels very much in the background, softened by the more lively scenes of palms, sand, and sea. The old memories of anniversary getaways and the new memories of "Nana's Family Vacay" co-exist together, inhabiting the same space.

It reminds me of my new old ring, the ring Jay gave me for our tenth wedding anniversary, the ring I loved so much that I chose to wear it as my wedding band for the next twenty-three years. I adored the subtle elegance of it: a simple band with ten tiny diamonds embedded in it. Even after our marriage fell apart, I couldn't look at this ring without feeling affection for it and remembering the night Jay gave it to me.

It was two months after April was born, and I was beyond exhausted, caring for a newborn while also tending to a toddler and a preschooler. But we wanted to celebrate the milestone of a decade of marriage, so I rallied and we hired a babysitter and made a reservation for dinner at the Chart House. Jay couldn't wait to give me the ring, told me later his plan was to surprise me over dessert and champagne, but his excitement couldn't be contained, and he presented it to me over our salads.

Surprised and delighted, I loved it immediately. Jay was a man of few words, but I felt like this ring was his way of saying, "I see you. I see us. I see our life together, and I love it."

I guess that's why I have always loved this ring so much. It reminds me of a time when I felt like he really did see me. A time when he really did love our life together, loving one another in the midst of loving and caring for these beautiful little souls we had brought into the world.

After we started the divorce process, I had a hard time letting go of the ring. I finally took it off sometime after I moved to Heron Dunes and laid it in the bottom of my jewelry box. I knew I couldn't wear it anymore, yet I kept it all the same. It reminded me, when I was tempted to think otherwise, that it wasn't all a sham, this love of ours, this marriage of complete opposites. There was a lot of good in there. This ring reminded me of the good. And after my grandchildren started coming, an idea was born in my heart.

Why not let this ring be transformed into something new, something that shows the beauty that might endure in the midst of loss?

So I decided to replace five of the ten diamonds with the birthstones of my five grandchildren.

I'm living a new story now. But I've come to realize this new story cannot be separated from the old story. It comes out of the old story, just like my grandchildren come from my children, who come from my marital union with their father. As much as I have wanted to leave the old story behind, leave my old self behind, I've come to accept that she is always with me. Whether I keep her in the shadows or not, she is still there.

So I feel like my new (old) ring is an emblem of my desire to invite my old story to take up space in my new story, to be a conscious participant in my ongoing journey toward wholeness. It's taken a good, long while to get here. I wasn't sure it would ever happen or that I would ever want it to. But slowly, over time, and with a lot of hard work, I have come to find myself in this place.

Letting these new stones sit right next to the old stones—each new stone alternating, interfacing, with each old one—feels like I am letting my new life make room for my old life. Letting my new story breathe life into my old story. Letting who I am now befriend who I was then. Gently reaching for her hand and saying, "Come along. Let's walk together. You belong here too."

Epilogue

She Is the Universe

Thread of Light: Recognize the sacred in your life

My friends have assorted names for her. Katy calls her
Great Mother. Beth calls her Strength of My Heart.
Sandra, who wrote a book about her, calls her Sophia.[1] She is
the feminine face of God, the divine feminine. The ancient
sacred texts from my faith tradition refer to her as Wisdom, the
one who dwelt with her people, who "guided them along a
marvelous way, and became a shelter to them by day, and a
starry flame through the night."[2] When I look back over my life,
I see threads of her presence all along the way: dwelling with
me, guiding me, sheltering me.

When my children were young, we went to see the Disney
movie *Pocahontas*. I was mesmerized by Grandmother Willow,
the ancient tree that spoke wisdom into Pocahontas's heart. I
began to imagine God as a warm and rooted grandmother,

rather than a stodgy, standoffish grandfather. I began to pray to Grandmother God rather than Heavenly Father.

I know grandmothers can be distant and judgmental and grandfathers can be generous and kind. It can be problematic to think of feminine characteristics as positive and masculine characteristics as negative, so I want to be careful not to delineate along those lines. God encompasses both genders and transcends gender. Embracing the feminine side of God has the potential to be an expansion of *both/and* rather than a choosing of *either/or*.

As Shannon Evans, author of *The Mystics Would Like a Word*, writes:

> Engaging with the feminine face of God does not mean obliterating the masculine one. Not only is there room for both in our spiritual imaginations but Julian of Norwich would argue that there's room for both *at the same time*. Dame Julian approached gender binaries playfully, with a refreshing absence of precision. She repeatedly wrote things like "Jesus births," "he mothers," and "Jesus as both Son and Mother," knowing in full confidence that the One who whispered the world into existence does not conform to gender binaries established by human society.[3]

Julian's words are echoed by my friend Sandra's conviction that "Jesus was such a man who held the sacred feminine in his soul."[4]

The challenge for me has been the way patriarchal cultures, from biblical times until present day, have interpreted God's character and God's activity in the world through their own lens of domineering control, which, at the very least, minimizes women and, at the very worst, legitimizes harm to women. Because of this, it can be all too easy to succumb to the notion that God is patriarchal too.

Perhaps this is why, initially, I couldn't hear God calling me into ministry. I recall my nightmare of a dream, where I was preaching in my home church and every single face staring back at me was my father's. The idea of saying yes to that did not feel safe. But then my dream of standing by a hospital bed ministering to a patient gave me a glimpse of the God who would come alongside me, nurturing me as I nurtured others. I longed to bear witness to that kind of God.

Evans writes that, unlike Julian of Norwich, "We are constantly filtering our theology through what we consider to be permissible. . . . We tend to defer to precedent rather than follow the nudgings of our own souls. We trust those in authority more than we trust ourselves."[5]

Filtering my theology, deferring to precedent, and trusting those in authority had all been true of my story. But as I began the journey of learning to trust myself and follow the nudging of my own soul, I realized I needed images that reflected my experience of God, not just my knowledge of God handed down to me from a hierarchy of men. "A Mighty Fortress Is Our God" no longer worked for me.

I needed images that reflected a God who was as near as my very breath, like a nursing mother with her infant child.[6] A God who gives birth to us,[7] who gathers us into her arms and keeps us safe, the way a hen gathers her brood under her wings.[8] A God who would show up at the bedside of a young mother in ICU.

During my time in seminary, I remember being in a small group and the group leader posing a question to those of us sitting with him in a circle.

"What is your earliest memory of God?" he asked us.

At first, the question made me uncomfortable. I didn't grow up going to church, didn't come to faith until I was a teenager, so I wasn't sure I had any recollection of God from an early age. But as people in the group began to share, I realized I had interpreted the question differently than they did. I was trying to figure out when I first *learned* about God, but the others in the group were sharing when they first *encountered* God. It was a question about experience, not knowledge.

As I sat there listening to my peers' stories, I was reminded of my early years with my paternal grandmother. Although my family didn't go to church when I was a little girl, almost every summer we traveled back home to my grandmother's cotton farm in North Louisiana, where I went with her to the old country church down the road. I thought of that church as God's house, but I instinctively knew God didn't hang out only there. She followed my grandmother everywhere she went.

Mamaw was my first memory of unconditional love—someone who kept me safe, wrapping her warm, loving arms around me and enfolding me into her bosom just because she delighted in my presence. I used to think I was her favorite, until I realized she loved her other eleven grandchildren the same way she loved me. I was awed by the way her love was expansive enough to include us all.

Mamaw embodied an up-close, not-afraid-to-get-her-hands-dirty kind of God. She nourished me with fried chicken and biscuits, saved me from the black snake slithering too close for comfort, and forgave me when I hid my black-eyed peas—the ones she had grown, picked, shelled, and boiled—in my iced tea because I didn't like the mealy way they tasted. She even cared about the dogs, gathering the scraps from our plates and setting them outside in a pie tin for the strays that came around. I knew in the marrow of my bones that Mamaw's God loved me. In the deepest part of my spirit, I knew I was lovable.

As I leaned into embracing the feminine side of God, I began to see how the divine feminine was present with me throughout my life. She was like a mustard seed within me, planting a whisper of an idea, a notion of a nudge. And then, somehow, when I offered my subtle nod of assent, my willingness to participate, these small gestures became growing, living things that suffused my life into something new.

This is why I like to think of her clothed in green, like the grass of the fields and the leaves on the trees. Alive, growing, fertile. For me, she is what twelfth-century Hildegard of Bingen called *viriditas*, "the greening power of God, the life force at work in all of creation."[9] This feels like a vividly fitting description of my experience with her.

As I look back, I see how she was there, not only embodied in the warm embrace of my grandmother, but also in the heart of the kind librarian who nurtured my love for reading. That cozy little library was a sanctuary for me before I ever knew what that word meant.

During my early running years, I believe she was the encouragement that rose up within my spirit, the voice of my inner knowing, saying, "You can do this." *You can do the hard things that will lead to your empowerment.* And "You don't have to do this." *You don't have to do the things that will lead to your diminishment.*

She was Mother Earth, reminding me of my sacred connection and worth. *You may be mere dust, but you are connected to a universe that celebrates dust, that grows new life out of the dirt every single day.*

She was my advocate when I advocated for Baby Meredith, showing me how to use my voice. She was the compassion of my counselor, helping to heal my broken spirit, and the wisdom within my bones, helping to heal my broken body. She was the whisper of my vocation, calling me home even as she called me to be a home for others. She was the sustaining love that knit my family together in a new way after my marriage fell apart.

She was the guidance of the moon, the beauty of the sunset, the wind that swept over the ocean waters and into my grief-filled heart. She was the generosity of spirit embodied in my neighbors, opening a window so hope could find a way in. She was the joy that woke up inside me, wooing me to embrace the fullness of my being and my life.

I've often wondered if perhaps she was present in the spirit of that beleaguered little armadillo that I saved from drowning, the one who saved me too. My friend Debbie Grace passed on some wisdom she found about the symbolism of armadillos:

> The armadillo's ability to thrive in various environments makes it a symbol of resilience and adaptability. As a spirit animal, it inspires individuals to remain steadfast in the face of adversity and to find creative solutions to overcome challenges.[10]

I remember that day. How my mindset shifted after saving that creature. How I was reminded that I am resourceful and resilient. That truth stayed with me, strengthening me, as I tackled the hard things that lay ahead.

I have a framed print in my bedroom of an ancient, expansive woman embracing a young girl, breathing her spirit upon her. In this image I see someone who is both rooted in this world and beyond it. The artist, Catherine Nagy Mowry, titled her painting *She Is the Universe, We Are Her Grandchildren.* When I look at *She Is the Universe* every night before I go to bed, I fall asleep knowing I am encircled within her Great Love.

And now I have discovered another name for her. She is the Befriender of My Story, the befriender of all my younger selves, the breath that breathes light into my spirit, redeeming what was lost and revealing the beauty and goodness that endure.

However she is known, she has been saving me all my life. And she is saving me still.

Notes

Chapter 4. My Body Knew

1. Terry Tempest Williams, *Refuge: An Unnatural History of Family and Place*, as quoted in Maria Popova, "On Change and Denial," *The Marginalian*, June 16, 2024, https://www.themarginalian.org/2024/06/18/terry-tempest-williams-refuge-change-denial/?mc_cid=83c6b57df1.

2. Laurie Frankel, *This Is How It Always Is* (New York: Flatiron Books, 2017), 65.

3. See John 5:2–7.

4. Hillary L. McBride, *The Wisdom of Your Body: Finding Healing, Wholeness, and Connection Through Embodied Living* (Grand Rapids, MI: Brazos Press, 2021), 63.

5. John E. B. Myers, *A Mother's Nightmare—Incest: A Practical Legal Guide for Parents and Professionals* (Thousand Oaks, CA: Sage Publications, 1997), 20.

Chapter 5. My Three Dreams

1. See Genesis 18:12.

2. Parker Palmer, *Let Your Life Speak: Listening for the Voice of Vocation* (San Francisco: Jossey-Bass, 2000), 16.

3. Natalie Goldberg, *The True Secret of Writing: Connecting Life With Language* (New York: Atria Paperback, 2013), xvi.

Chapter 7. Sanctuary by the Sea

1. Maggie Smith, *You Could Make This Place Beautiful* (New York: One Signal Publishers/Atria, 2023), 257.

2. Learn more about Daniele at www.danieleevans.org.

3. Kathy Swaar, *Fine Lines: Walking the Labyrinth of Grief and Loss* (pub. by author, 2021), 135.

4. Jillian Kramer, "Sheryl Sandberg Reveals the Daily Practice That Helped Boost Her Spirits After Her Husband's Death," Glamour.com, December 30, 2015, https://www.glamour.com/story/sheryl-sandberg-this-is-my-new.

5. Jan Richardson, "Walking the Way of Hope: A Retreat for Women's Christmas," 2017, http://sanctuaryofwomen.com/WomensChristmasRetreat2017.pdf, 37.

6. See www.bookwifery.com for more information about Christianne's book services.

7. See www.acontemplativelight.com for more information about the Light House.

Chapter 8. Two Little Lights

1. David Nicholls, *You Are Here* (New York: Harper Collins, 2024), 140.

2. Maggie Smith, *Keep Moving: Notes on Loss, Creativity,*

and Change (New York: One Signal Publishers/Atria, 2020), 105.

3. Ross Gay, *Inciting Joy* (Chapel Hill, NC: Algonquin Books of Chapel Hill, 2022), 4.

Epilogue

1. Sandra Logan, *Sophia's Way: Wisdom's Dance With the Feminine Soul* (pub by author, 2021).

2. Wisdom of Solomon 10:17; see also Sirach 24:8–12.

3. Shannon K. Evans, *The Mystics Would Like a Word*, as quoted in Center for Action and Contemplation, "Julian of Norwich: Weekly Summary and Expanding Images Practice," August 17, 2024, https://cac.org/daily-meditations/julian-of-norwich-weekly-summary/.

4. Logan, *Sophia's Way*, viii.

5. Evans, https://cac.org/daily-meditations/julian-of-norwich-weekly-summary/.

6. See Isaiah 49:15.

7. See Deuteronomy 32:18.

8. See Matthew 23:37.

9. Christine Valters Paintner, *Illuminating the Way: Embracing the Wisdom of Monks and Mystics* (Notre Dame, IN: Sorin Books, 2016), 161.

10. Critter Stop, "Armadillo Symbolism: Understanding the Meaning and Significance," https://critterstop.com/post/armadillo-symbolism-understanding-the-meaning-and-significance/.

Acknowledgments

When I think about all the people who have surrounded me in this writing endeavor, I am reminded once again that while the act of putting pen to paper (or fingers to keyboard) is a solitary activity, the writing process is suffused with support from so many different sources.

To my editor, Christianne Squires, thank you for saying yes to working on a second book together. Your expertise, guidance, and compassion have made this experience enjoyable and affirming, even in the midst of the stress. I know for certain that because of you, this book is the best possible version of itself.

To the women of my writers' group, Kathryn Coneway and Noelle Rollins, thank you for your companionship, encouragement, and accountability on this journey. I would still be working on this project, nowhere near finished, if not for you. You have pushed me to go deeper into my stories than I would have gone myself, and I am so grateful for it. Because of you, this book is much more robust than what I imagined it could be.

To the women of the Bookwifery Collective (Anne Brock, Kathryn Coneway, Janice Gutierrez, Kathy Swaar, Cindy Van

Lunen, and Jennifer Willhoite), thank you for our weekly gatherings over the years, for being a sounding board, for celebrating with me as I crossed milestones and commiserating with me when I hit stumbling blocks. The essence of the spirit of our group is infused in this book.

To the women of my weekly examen group (Anne Brock, Kathryn Coneway, Elisabeth Fuchs, Kate Lillie, Noelle Rollins, and Jennifer Willhoite), I am so grateful for the way I am seen by each of you. The way you bear witness to my life has given me courage to pursue this project.

To the women of the Light House community, I am so grateful to be surrounded by a sisterhood of kindred spirits. The way each of you bear your light in the world has inspired me to listen more deeply to the way this book wants to be a light for others.

Writing this book, diving down into the stories of my life, brought me close to those who brought light and love to my younger selves, and I want to express my gratitude for them.

For three friends, Dana Meadows Soltis, Sherry McElveen, and Missy Hart, who befriended my younger selves and made all the difference in who I am. Dana and I were in the same grade in high school. She befriended me after Jay left for college and I began my junior year feeling all alone. We were both on the cross-country team, and after I left the team, Dana often met up with me to run together. My second summer working on the farm, Dana joined me there as a fellow stand girl. We were bridesmaids in each other's weddings. I'm so grateful to you, Dana, for befriending my young self, for really seeing me, and for drawing me into your circle of warmth and laughter.

Sherry McElveen and I met through a church-related event when I was thirty-three years old. She was there through the mysterious medical issues, the surgeries, the memories, the estrangement, the therapy, and beyond. Ten years my senior, she was a spiritual mentor for me. We began meeting weekly for breakfast to sit with one another and inquire "How is it with your soul?" This was a practice we continued for more than twenty years. Thank you, Sherry, for befriending my younger self, for nurturing my spirit and helping me to claim my identity as Beloved.

Missy Hart and I met during a seminary class the summer I turned forty-one, and recognizing a kindred spirit in one another, we soon became good friends. We spent hours conversing about a more hopeful and inclusive theology, and once we both graduated, we became covenant partners in ministry, affirming and encouraging one another through all the ups and downs of living out our vocational callings. Thank you, Missy, for befriending my younger self, for believing in me, for reminding me who I am when I was prone to forget.

For Linda and Stewart Barlow, friends whom Jay and I met when I was pregnant with April, who not only befriended us but embraced our children too. I will be forever grateful for your friendship to me as a young mother, for the way you have loved my children, and for the enduring way you have continued to befriend me as a single person.

For my children, Wilson (and Bridget), Meredith (and Anthony), and April, thank you for never giving up on me. I hope this book sheds light on stories that may have lived in the shadows. More vitally, I hope it sheds light on how much I have always loved each of you.

And for my grandchildren, Isla, Charlotte, Elizabeth, Harlynne, and James, thank you for bringing so much love and light into my life. I love being your Nana. I hope this book will help you remember my story and what I want to pass on to each of you. May you always glimpse threads of light in your own stories.